A. James Gregor

REFLECTIONS ON ITALIAN FASCISM
An Interview with Antonio Messina

About the author:
A. James Gregor is Professor emeritus of Political Science at the University of California, Berkeley. He is the author of thirty-one books on political doctrine and intellectual history. He was a graduate, with Distinction in History, of Columbia University in New York; an Adjunct Lecturer for the Marine Corps University in Quantico; a Senior Fellow at the Institute for Advanced Study in the Social Sciences at Hebrew University, Jerusalem, Israel; and H. L. Oppenheimer Professor at the Marine Corps University, Quantico, Virginia. He has testified before both Houses of the United States Congress. He was awarded a Knighthood in the Order of Merit by the Republic of Italy.

Antonio Messina is a freelance journalist, a book agent, and a historian of the Fascist period.

A. James Gregor

REFLECTIONS ON ITALIAN FASCISM

An Interview with Antonio Messina

Logos Verlag Berlin

 λογος

Bibliographic information
published by the Deutsche Nationalbibliothek

The Deutsche Nationalbibliothek lists this publication in the
Deutsche Nationalbibliografie; detailed bibliographic data are
available on the Internet at http://dnb.d-nb.de .

ISBN 978-3-8325-4182-8

Logos Verlag Berlin GmbH
Comeniushof, Gubener Str. 47,
10243 Berlin
Germany
Tel.: +49 (0)30 42 85 10 90
Fax: +49 (0)30 42 85 10 92
http://www.logos-verlag.com

To my wife
– Maria Hsia Chang –
for all the years

Author's Introduction

The interview before the reader was prompted by political developments in the Middle East and the direct impact those developments have had in both Europe and the United States. "Jihadism," the armed expression of extremist Islamism, has precipitated a displacement of populations unparalleled since the end of the Second World War. The flood of migrants and refugees has taxed the resources and the response capabilities of all the nations of Europe. Part of the reaction has been a measureable shift to the political right in a variety of places. In some cases there has been significant resistance to the admission of migrants attended by real or potential violence. The media has been quick to identify these occurrences as "a rise of fascism."

In the United States, both the violence of jihadist extremists as well as the reaction by anti-jihadist elements have similarly been characterized as "fascist." Together with those marginal persons who bomb government buildings, set fire to abortion facilities, vandalize gravestones in Jewish cemeteries, and use politically offensive speech, they are all deemed "fascist."

One of the results has been that several European journalists have requested an interview with me in order to discuss the putative return of a political ideology presumably destroyed by force of arms in the Second World War. As a political scientist I have spent the bulk of my academic career in the study of Fascism – that revolutionary system identified with Benito Mussolini that dominated Italian and influenced European politics for the first half of the twentieth century. It was a movement and an ideology presumably destroyed in the most devastating war in human history.

And yet, for years after its purported demise, evidences of fascism have continued to surface virtually everywhere. The term "fascism" has become one of generic abuse, invoked to elicit repugnance. As a term employed in ordinary speech, it has become all but entirely emotive in content, offering little, if any, cognitive substance. Very few among us would venture on an effort to define "fascism" – as it was in its time, or as it is understood in our own.

When Mr. Antonio Messina approached me with the suggestion that an interview on the subject of "Italian Fascism" might help to resolve some of the confusions that have collected around the subject and that currently seemed to occupy more and more of our attention, I agreed. Historic Fascism was one of the major political forces of the twentieth century – and it has continued to influence our world in a variety of ways. Not only has it become an inextricable part of our political vocabulary, but traces of its doctrine can, in fact, be found in a variety of places. To follow its influence over more than half a century – and to identify its real presence – requires retracing its sometimes obscure passage from one time to another. I have tried to accomplish this with a minimum of academic jargon. The text before the reader was intended for an intelligent lay audience. For my colleagues who would like more academic references for my opinions I have provided a list of my publications dealing with each and every aspect of the political phenomena dealt with in the interview.

The interview is intended to deliver a coherent account of Fascism – its rise on the Italian peninsula, its military defeat in the Second World War, and its survival in the political behaviors of those revolutionaries responding to economic, political, and psychological stimuli reminiscent of those that gave rise to the paradigmatic form. The interview is offered as a summary recounting of sixty years of academic research. It is hoped that it will help to clarify a considerable portion of the radical politics of the late twentieth and the early twenty-first centuries.

A. James Gregor
Berkeley, California
December 2015

Preface by Anthony J. Joes

A. James Gregor is an internationally acknowledged authority on the subject of totalitarian political systems – with emphasis on Fascism and "fascisms." In the interview below, Professor Gregor demonstrates his familiarity with every aspect of Fascism – its history, philosophy, applications, as well as those national forms that, at times, are classified as variants. He traces linkages between ideas and phenomena that previously might have seemed unrelated. He makes a case, for example, that some East European, and East Asian, states are, or have been, "fascist" in all but name.

His fundamental ideas on Italian Fascism are so clear, so persuasive, and so well documented in his earlier works, that they can be convincingly summarized with brevity in the interview herewith provided. First, and perhaps foremost, he rejects conflating Italian Fascism with Hitler's National Socialism. Mussolini's association with Hitler in the closing years of the 1930s, can be traced to the clear possibility that Germany appeared to be poised to dominate Europe for years, if not decades. Mussolini feared that if Italy did not become Hitler's ally, it would become his vassal. The case is made that Italian Fascism was a revolutionary movement independent of Hitler's National Socialism, and their association in the Second World War was the result of contingent circumstances.

Gregor argues that Fascism was a form of reactive nationalism, responding to felt humiliation at the hands of nations more economically advanced. If it were to seek political equality and prosper in the competitive environment of the twentieth century, Italy would be compelled to rapidly develop its industrial economy. Nationalism and rapid eco-

11

nomic development became the dominant political "myths" of the system. In committing itself to the program entailed in such commitments, Fascist Italy became the paradigm of revolution for nations that found themselves in similar circumstances throughout the century. For Gregor, that helps to explain why "fascist" features are to be found in the revolutionary movements of economically less developed communities that insist on their "Marxism" or "socialism." In some instances, their "fascist" features are pronounced: the state dominates the political system, the unitary party controls both it and the economy, and the charismatic leadership infuses it all with an ideology conceived impeccable.

The interview is filled with illuminating suggestions. The reading would profit both the political science professional as well as the intelligent lay reader. It is recommended to those who study politics as well as those who are interested in our potential future.

Anthony James Joes
Professor emeritus of Political Science
Saint Joseph's University

The interview

*You have studied Italian Fascism for more than half a century,
could you tell us something about the circumstances surrounding your study during that period?*

Italian Fascism was among those subjects to which I devoted my academic attention since the end of the Second
World War. By the time I undertook my studies, the academic domain of "revolutionary politics" had been divided
into two discrete divisions: the Left and the Right. How
that came about is a tale that is much too long to tell.
Nonetheless, at my very first exposure, I found that somehow Italian Fascism had been irretrievably categorized as of
the "radical Right." That was followed by a varying list of
properties understood to define such movements. In the literature made available to lay persons, the Right, as a class of
political phenomena was broadly defined as "reactionary,"
"genocidal," and generally "inhumane." The more sophisticated academic literature was not quite as crude, but it was
clear that the popular judgments were derivative of those
given expression by the more professional.

Fascism was depicted as an exemplar of the Right. Peter
Nathan's *The Psychology of Fascism* typified the entire class
of available literature. Older books like Wilhelm Reich's
The Mass Psychology of Fascism appeared in new editions.
These were supplemented by works like *The Authoritarian
Personality* that exploited the newer "behavioristic" trends
in social science. All pointed to the unique disabilities that
afflicted both individual "fascists" as well as the "masses"
that were to provide its base. Sigmund Neuman's *Perma-
nent Revolution: The Total State in a World at War* argued that fascists were inevitably "lonely" and "insecure,"
impairments that made them "rootless" and "explosively ni-

hilistic." Workers were found in the ranks of Fascism because of their "disillusionment," and the middle class enlisted because it felt threatened by the class struggle anticipated by socialism.

All of this was supplemented by a republication of R. Palme Dutt's prewar *Fascism and Social Revolution* in which we were told that Fascism was a "tool of high finance" or of a "combined dictatorship of agrarian and industrial capital." While most academics were not prepared to accept the omnibus generalizations of the Marxist-Leninist interpretation of Fascism, much of the pervasive sentiment, enhanced by the emotions of the recent war, found expression in the classrooms of postwar America. Only with the appearance of "revisionist" works like that of Ernst Nolte and Renzo De Felice did some members of the academic community choose to review the credibility of the prevailing interpretations of Fascism.

The entire issue had been still further confounded by the prevailing disposition to identify Italian Fascism with National Socialist Germany. It was decided that whatever could be said of Hitler's National Socialism, could be said, without qualification, of Mussolini's Fascism. Allied propaganda during the Second World War had fused the two regimes into one objectionable political phenomenon. As a consequence, the culpability for all the innocent dead of the death camps could be deposited at the feet of generic "fascists." All the monstrous crimes and moral obscenities that attended the prosecution of the war could be charged to an omnibus "fascism" – a concept that covered, without distinction, both Mussolini's Fascism and Hitler's National Socialism. Only years after the termination of the war did

De Felice's documented distinction between Italian Fascism and the Nazism of Adolf Hitler argue a qualitative difference between the two. While many established scholars were comfortable with the prevailing and convenient interpretation of "fascism" born of the war, many younger scholars began to suspect the credibility of identifying the two systems. That bred a skepticism that led some to question the neat distinction between Right and Left revolutionaries – with the Right monstrous in ideology and effect, and the Left humane and progressive.

By that time Carl Friedrich and Zbigniew K. Brzezinski published their *Totalitarian Dictatorship and Autocracy*, signaling the advent of the "cold war" – in the course of which more and more scholars proceeded to perceive "socialist dictatorships" as evil as any "fascist" power. That altered the dimensions of the interpretation of Italian Fascism. In fact, Hannah Arendt's *The Origins of Totalitarianism* went so far as to deny that Mussolini's Fascism was totalitarian at all. The landscape of "fascist studies" had been forever transformed. There were "bad" regimes – all "totalitarian" – and there were less- or non-offensive regimes. Italian Fascism, as an authoritarianism, was identified as less offensive than the totalitarian regimes of Hitler, Stalin, and Mao Zedong. To the students of totalitarianism that made Italian Fascism less interesting, but it also allowed Mussolini's regime to be studied dispassionately – with more emphasis on objective evidence than mimetic compliance with prevailing prejudice.

In retrospect, it seems to have been the case that academics were prepared to argue that the intention of any totalitarian system would be absolute control – and irrespective of Arendt's judgments – Italian Fascism was deemed totalitarian. In that context one might study Italian Fascism with a certain degree of detachment. Everyone agreed that total control could hardly be achieved in the real world. Stalin certainly did not have absolute control of his system. Neither did Hitler – nor Mao Zedong. They all exercised different degrees of control; but the fact that they all sought such extensive control is what is of significance – not that any achieved total control. In all such systems, the state controls more aspects of private lives than is conceivable in nontotalitarian environments. The extent and character of that control varied with each system. Clearly, in the Fascist case, convinced as they were that the existence of some degree of private property, and some private associations, were functionally desirable (given the influence of economic theorists like Vilfredo Pareto and Maffeo Pantaleoni), their program of rapid industrial development allowed institutions that antedated the Great War to survive (again, controlled in large measure by state and party intervention).

Among the traditional institutions allowed to survive was the Roman Catholic Church. Any attempt to suppress the Church would have so many deleterious consequences that Mussolini conceived its control (through the Lateran Accords, for example) the more advisable course. A similar argument was made for the continued survival of the monarchy and the military.

The fact that Fascism was "syncretic," allowing pre-Fascist economic, monarchial, religious, and military institutions to survive the revolution, was largely a function of the political circumstances in which it rose to power. Mussolini had observed that what was required to expunge those institutions in Lenin's Russia included the almost total collapse of the Russian economy, a protracted civil war, and the starvation and murder of millions. Rather than pay that price, disabling the rapid economic development he intended, Mussolini chose to control such nonfascist institutions through state and party intervention. Should one choose to call such a system "administered," rather than "totalitarian," it becomes little more than a matter of preference.

The entire discussion of totalitarianism, at a time when the sentiments of the recent war were receding into the past, allowed for illuminating distinctions to be considered. More and more documents and testimonies surfaced, and the interpretation of an entire epoch grew increasingly nuanced. The study of the revolutionary movements of the interwar, and wartime, years became illuminated by reasonable objectivity. It was an exciting period for scholars. There were many, like myself, who took a renewed interest in the suppressed realities of the past. Armed with the magnificent training we received in historiography, sociology, and political science, we could reexamine the past with some measure of detachment and refreshed intensity, free from the stultifying passions of war.

There was, of course, resistance. Those scholars, who had grown comfortable with the convenience of identifying "fascism" as a union of Italian Fascism and National Socialism, were loath to surrender it to the new dispensation. When the concept of "totalitarianism" suggested that the concept covered regimes on the Left as well as the Right, many academicians, committed as they were to the Left, refused to acknowledge any similarity between a Marxist system and "fascism." They simply refused to consider the fact that the Soviet mass murder of innocents and the Maoist homicidal abuse of workers were as egregious as the mass murders attributed to Hitler's Nazism. That coupled with the fact that there was little mass murder in Mussolini's Italy was simply unacknowledged. There were enough instances of political suppression and incarceration for political offenses in Fascist Italy to allow committed scholars on the Left to continue to speak of Italian Fascism as a "misanthropic totalitarianism." To this day, unregenerate Leftists continue to speak of "fascism" when they, in fact, mean National Socialism. Nonetheless, by the late 1960s, for those who respond to public evidence, the identification of Italian Fascism with National Socialism could no longer be insisted upon without significant qualification.

Could you tell us something of your training and your instructors?

The bulk of my formal training was undertaken at Columbia University in New York City in the immediate postwar years. My training included the standard preparation for historical studies – establishing evidence of the veridicality of documents, the confirmation of data, and the plausibility of interpretation. That was supplemented by studies in the philosophy of social science. Professor Arthur Danto was particularly influential in both these areas – as was Professor Paul Oskar Kristeller. My special study of social science was under the guidance of Professors Sidney Morgenbesser and Paul Lazarsfeld, both notable in the field. Professor Kristeller was to have a peculiar influence on my studies. He happened to have had experience in both National Socialist

Germany and Fascist Italy. He was of Jewish extraction and therefore brought special insights into the subject with which I had become increasingly interested.

It was Professor Kristeller who informed me of the vast difference between the National Socialism of Adolf Hitler's Germany and Mussolini's Fascism. Kristeller had fled Germany because the anti-Semitic legislation there precluded his further teaching. He became a resident in Italy and was sheltered by Giovanni Gentile. He told me of the political circumstances in Italy and of the availability of sanctuary. He spoke of working with Italians in an environment of acceptance. He told me that the political climate there was fundamentally different from that of National Socialist Germany. When Fascist Italy adopted anti-Semitism (for evident political reasons), he was forced to leave, to migrate to the United States. Once there, he continued to be very eloquent about the differences between the two regimes – irrespective of the fact that eventually he was forced to leave Italy. He spoke vaguely of the political compromises that Fascism had made – but it was clear that he still acknowledged the deep differences between Fascism and National Socialism. He suggested I read the Fascist literature available in the Paterno Library (in the Casa Italiana) located on campus. It was there I discovered an enormous trove of literature devoted to the politics of revolutionary Italy. It was there I found the writings of A. O. Olivetti and Sergio Panunzio, for example – and that of the Italian Nationalists like Enrico Corradini and Alfredo Rocco. I had never heard of any of these political ideologists. (Years later a prominent scholar confided that the reason not much Fascist doctrinal literature could be found was because there was hardly any – there were very few Fascists who could write books or articles!) Needless to say, I was familiar (as were all American college students) with Marx and the multitude of Marxists who were to follow – but I was completely innocent of any knowledge of the Italian literature relevant to the development of Fascist thought. The fact is that once I immersed myself in that literature, it struck me not only as interesting and illuminating, but immediately suggestive of an alternative interpretation of Italian Fascism.

From that point on I read more and more of the pre-Fascist and Fascist doctrinal literature – and decided that I would write a kind of intellectual history of Italian Fascism. By that time I was absolutely convinced that fundamental ideological differences separated the two Axis partners – and whatever might be said of one could not automatically be said of the other. The situation was somewhat similar between the United States and the Soviet Union. The United States and the Soviet Union were allied in the war – and yet they were separated by an unbridgeable ideological gulf. During the war the United States rarely, if ever, alluded to those differences – and yet they were there. Washington made no objection to the Soviet abolition of private property in the territory it occupied – and we witnessed the Soviet murder of thousands of Polish military officers at the commencement of the Soviet ground war in Poland. We said nothing because the Soviets were our ally in a time of existential threat. I came to understand that. None of that made the United States the same as the Soviet Union. Similarly, Fascist Italy apparently considered it prudent to assume postures that would reduce the distance between Fascism and National Socialism – in order to render their security alliance truly "totalitarian." That did not make Fascism indistinguishable from National Socialism.

By the time of the onset of the "cold war," a recognition of all that led me to examine the ideological rationale of all the revolutionary movements of the twentieth century – with particular emphasis on the Left/Right distinction. By that time the academic community was prepared to acknowledge that Stalinism had mercilessly exploited the workers and peasants of the Soviet Union. Millions had been forced to labor in unspeakable conditions. Millions died. Government policy had caused famine and the death of still further millions. At the same time, the bureaucratic classes prospered. Such a system could hardly be identified as a "Marxist workers' government" that was supposed to be the product of the traditional revolutionary Left. The persistent disposition among researchers to divide revolutionary movements along a Left/Right divide no longer seemed tenable. Like many others, I began to search for other, more plausible descriptive categories into which the revolutionary movements of those times might be incorporated. I did not intend to write a *history* of those times – I thought I might provide some sort of an introductory account of the *ideas* that influenced that history. My publications, *A Survey of Marxism* and *Contemporary Radical Ideologies*, followed.

Of the ideologies I studied, I found that of Fascist Italy most interesting – for a variety of reasons. I became increasingly convinced that I should attempt to provide a reasonable account of its doctrine. Except for a few notable prewar books, there was almost nothing that delivered an account of Fascist ideology that actually made recourse to Fascist doctrinal literature. (Many Anglophone academicians had convinced themselves that it would be a singular piece of foolishness to spend time reading Fascist doctrinal literature – since they intuitively knew what Fascism was *really* about!) Very few of the authors who wrote "interpretations" of Fascism at that time were in the least familiar with its primary doctrinal literature.

To this day there are some academicians who argue that Fascism was animated exclusively by two values: "violence and war." Only by dismissing the significance of the voluminous Fascist literature available might anyone allow themselves to say something so obviously untrue. One could read the dozens of volumes written by Giovanni Gentile, for example, when he served as the philosopher of Fascism, and not find a single quote that would testify to the Fascist unqualified commitment to violence and war.[1] Recognizing the vacuity of the claim, others have selected other values understood to typify Fascism. Rarely have they documented their selection by reference to the available Fascist doctrinal literature. It is a style of exposition that clearly gives expression to prejudgment. During the "cold war," similar strategies were employed in the exposition of "Marxist thought" by its committed opponents. "Values" were attributed to "Marxists" that were hardly found in the doctrinal literature of communism. Since they *intuitively knew* what Marxists believe, such committed scholarship found it unnecessary to document assertions with references to the actual doctri-

---

[1] The practice was to reject doctrinal pronouncements and insist that it was not what fascists *said*, but what they *did,* that was determinative. Of course, the practitioners' reports of what Fascists did almost always seemed to conform to what was expected.

nal literature. In both cases, the efforts were flawed. They speak to stultifying bias, and irrepressible prejudgment.

At the time of your initial studies, how would you characterize the state of "fascist studies" in your country?

When I began my serious study of Fascism, the discipline had been constructed around descriptive categories. "Fascism" was typically understood to cover both the political system of Mussolini's Italy and Hitler's National Socialist Germany. Sometimes the scope was more generous – determined by the descriptive category used to identify members of the class. If the descriptive category was "authoritarianism," it might include political systems that were basically or simply unrepresentative or antidemocratic. Sometimes the anticommunist and fundamentally monarchial system of Francisco Franco, the conservative and religiously oriented Austria of Engelbert Dollfuss, the monarchial system of Admiral Miklós Horthy of Hungary, as well as the simple authoritarianism of Józef Pilsudski of Poland, were indiscriminately included in the class of "fascisms." There was little, if any, regard for making any finer distinctions. Being authoritarian and anti-communist seemed sufficient for entry into the class. Political systems that identified themselves as Marxist, although clearly "authoritarian," formed a class of their own. There was a tendency to consider Marxist systems as somehow fundamentally different. They were, for example, "protodemocratic" – as though such systems actually intended to be democratic but were inhibited by circumstances. The distinction was between Left- and Rightwing authoritarianism. It was somehow understood that the authoritarian systems of the Left really aspired to be democratic – while authoritarian systems of the Right were intrinsically antidemocratic. Having imposed a hard distinction between the Left and the Right, some researchers chose to refine the set of criteria employed in identifying "fascism." Dissatisfied with the loosely jointed collection of "fascisms," some sought to devise more discriminating categories under which "fascism" could be more responsibly housed. One of the defining properties attributed to "fascism" was its singularly *immoral* character. Generic fascism was seen as a product of a "moral crisis." In the recent past, the West was somehow understood to have lost its moral integrity. Benedetto Croce provided a considerable part of the impetus of such a characterization, and by the late 1960s it had been largely standardized by an interpretation of Peter Drucker's *The End of Economic Man*. The effort proved unsatisfactory for a number of reasons – but perhaps foremost was the acknowledgment that there was no generally accepted objective common standard of morality/immorality.

While such a classificatory system was very popular, the category "immoral authoritarianism" did not really deliver the specificity sought. In the first instance it clearly did not distinguish between "fascism" and nonfascist systems. By the 1950s many academicians were prepared to acknowledge that Marxist systems, among others, were both authoritarian and immoral. In fact, it was decided that the suitable category was neither authoritarian nor immoral, but "totalitarian."

That was not taken to mean that totalitarian systems were not also authoritarian or immoral. It just meant that Left-wing systems were just as likely to be authoritarian and immoral as Right-wing systems. But Hannah Arendt had insisted that Mussolini's Fascism was not sufficiently immoral to qualify as totalitarian. Granted that – could Fascism still qualify as "fascist"? Was it sufficiently immoral? If Fascism was not considered sufficiently immoral to qualify as totalitarian, just how immoral was it? Surely, there were occasions when Italian Fascism conducted itself in an indecent and immoral fashion. The real question is: Has there ever been a political system that has not? The United States, for example, while fighting "fascist racism" in the Second World War, was denying civil rights to one tenth of its citizen population because of their race! Blacks in the United State were denied some of their most fundamental citizen, as well as human, rights. For their part, the British were similarly violating the citizen and human rights of colonials throughout the Empire. Some have consistently argued that the economic system of the "plutocratic" powers – those powers industrially advanced – were both indecent and exploitative. Very often it appears that morality and/or immorality is in the eye of the beholder. The question is: Is immoral conduct, in one measure or other, a prerequisite to identification as "fascism"? If so, what is the measure? The fact is that "immorality" is not a category that is very useful in the comparative analysis of political systems. Must a political system be immoral in order the meet the entrance requirements as a "totalitarianism" or as a "fascism"?

For its part, the categorization "totalitarian" has shown itself to be useful for classificatory purpose. Very few analysts fail to acknowledge the family resemblance, in terms of institutional properties, between Italian Fascism, National Socialism, Stalinism, Maoism and the related single party systems, informed by an ideology considered impeccably true, and led by a "charismatic" of one sort or another. How "morality" or "immorality" enters into the equation is uncertain.

In the effort to identify a class of political systems as "fascist," quite independent of its membership in the categorization "totalitarian," others sought to distinguish them as systems that rested on the consent and participation of *irrational* masses. Generic fascism arose to power and consolidated its rule because it could marshal unthinking populations under its guidon.

Once again, quite independent of totalitarianism as a category, there were many political systems that could plausibly be characterized as immoral, authoritarian, and the products of mass mobilization. Some have argued that the industrially developed democracies are, and always have been, immoral, authoritarian, and dependent on the support of feckless masses gulled into supporting the system by public spectacles, distracting competitive games, and welfare inducements. Once again, the category appears to be far too generous; it seems potentially to include *every available* political configuration – democratic and antidemocratic, moral and immoral, multiparty and single party, as well as Left-wing and Right-wing.

Given these circumstances, Marxists sought to resolve the confusion by insisting there was one indefeasible research strategy that would identify "fascist" political systems. They sought to convince both academic and lay audiences that generic fascism was the product of *class struggle*. Whatever negative properties it displayed were the predictable consequence of the class struggle between those who dominate the economic system and those who are their victims. Marx had predicted that economic competition would drive the possessing classes and the working class further and further apart – until the conditions generated by commodity production inevitably would produce a situation in which "the vast majority" would find itself in such misery that the sole recourse was total and fundamental economic, social, and political revolution. The "immiseration" of the population was conceived inevitable – so too was the liberating revolution. Only the resistance of a small coterie of the propertied was anticipated. Fascism was considered the embodiment of that resistance.

Given that interpretation, generic fascism was conceived to be a mercenary force that acted in the armed defense of *capitalism* – in either its financial, agricultural, or industrial incarnation. Sometimes it was seen as serving as the armed defense of all three together. What resulted was the expectation that a catastrophic collapse of the economy would result in a political system that was authoritarian and immoral, that mobilized the forlorn masses of declining capitalism to the reactionary purpose of resisting their own liberation. This is a candidate interpretation that forever has been popular with the political and academic Left. The principal difficulty with it is that it is far too generous. It makes every system that involves commodity production in a competitive market a "fascism" or a potential "fascism." Only Marxist command economies, that have abolished private ownership of the means of production, are not, and cannot be, "fascist." Every other economic system is either "fascist" or potentially "fascist." All non-Marxist systems merge into one generous and all-encompassing "fascism." We are faced with the sociological analogue of a night in which all cats are black. Not the best occasion for discernment.

The Marxist interpretation of generic fascism had been popular since the late 1920s and early 1930s. By the 1960s, it had become a little shop-worn. While still popular among Left-wing academics, it was no longer the dominant interpretation. It was more generally part of a more eclectic account. "Fascism" was understood to be part of the class struggle, but it also was composed of mindless masses, of persons suffering serious psychological deficits, that generated among them an irrepressible immorality that led to homicidal rage. War and violence was the inevitable outcome.

By the mid-1960s all that had become increasingly implausible. Some prominent academicians, themselves, became "revisionists" – and revisionist literature became reasonably abundant.

If Fascist studies were in such an unsatisfactory state, how did you pursue your research?

The revisionist literature of the 1960s provided the impetus for work that I had already begun. By the beginning of the decade I had collected an extensive library of doctrinal literature, ranging from that left us by traditional Marxists, together with that of Leninists and syndicalists – supplemented by the writings of national syndicalists and revolutionary nationalists. Governed by what I understood to be the principles of responsible social science inquiry, I read as much as possible of the available material – in an effort to discover the "projects" that were revealed.

The reference to "projects" alludes to some collection of intentions revealed in the analysis of complex events – that permits a reasonably coherent understanding of what would otherwise by little more than impenetrable confusion. For those who had studied Italian Fascism, a number of such project terms had been suggested – all of which I, and most of the revisionists, found unsatisfactory. My reading suggested to me that Fascism was essentially *a mass mobilizing developmental system*. Its ideology gave explicit expression to its intentions. It presented itself as a revolutionary movement that had the rapid economic, and specifically industrial, development of the retrograde economy of the Italian peninsula as its "project". Around recognition of that project, an account of Fascism could be constructed that made the entire sequence of events, from its commencement to its conclusion, more comprehensible.

I had been brought to that conviction by the doctrinal literature of Fascism itself. Anyone who had read the revolutionary syndicalist literature of those with whom Mussolini had interacted in the decade prior to the Great War – would have read Olivetti's acknowledgment that traditional Marxism had no answers for communities that had not reached the level of industrial maturity required for a truly Marxist revolution.

Like many of the syndicalists of the period, Olivetti recognized that the revolutionary program of traditional Marxism failed to address the problems of then contemporary Italy. Olivetti reminded his readers that Marx had insisted that his revolution required the realization of a set of necessary prerequisites before the intended liberation was possible. One of the principal prerequisites of the social revolution was that the vast majority of the population of a community in crisis be composed of "proletarians." That prerequisite "vast majority" would have to be composed of workers who had become inured to the responsibilities of production – who upon the advent of social revolution could assume control and direction of economic activity. Such proletarians could spontaneously take upon themselves the responsibilities of production. By the time of the War in Tripoli (1911) most serious Marxists – as syndicalists – recognized that Italy remained so backward that the nation's working population remained largely agrarian, a population the first Marxists had held to be "reactionary."

All of that impacted the politics of Italy's radicals of the Left. When the syndicalists had to face the reality of Italy's involvement in the war in Tripoli, Olivetti argued that because of Italy's backwardness, Marxist revolution was not an option. Instead, he maintained that true revolutionaries should identify with the national community in its effort to address the multiple burdens backwardness had imposed upon it. Olivetti conceived the war as focusing on the pre-capitalist state of the nation's economy, its resource shortfall, as well as the demographic stresses of the peninsula. In his judgment Italy was in pre-Marxist circumstances and in those circumstances, war had far different implications than it would have had Italy been industrially mature. In the course of his political analysis, Olivetti found himself agreeing with at least some of the assessment made by the nation's revolutionary nationalists.

Although clearly under the influence of the revolutionary syndicalists during this period, Mussolini resisted this first effort at the revolutionary revision of traditional Marxism, and remained an essentially "orthodox" revolutionary. He went on to become one of Italian socialism's foremost theorists and political leaders. The coming of the Great War was to change all that. The very outbreak of the conflict made it abundantly clear that the masses were inspired not by Marxism, but by *nationalism*.

Mussolini early became familiar with the strength of nationalist sentiment. He had served as a socialist agitator in the Italian speaking regions of Austria-Hungary in the period before the Great War – and, at that time, had defended Italian ethnicity against German pretentions. At the same time, he began his long association with Giovanni Prezzolini's *Vociani* – whose iconoclastic nationalism was a matter of common knowledge.

With the outbreak of the Great War, Mussolini found himself moved by a conviction that the conflict might very well determine the course of European history for decades after its conclusion. In his judgment, and the judgment of many of the Marxist "subversives" around him, the conflict gave evidence that it was to be a "revolutionary" war. By that time many syndicalists opted to support an Italian intervention in the war – as an ally of the Entente. To that purpose, Olivetti helped found the *Fascio rivoluzionario d'azione interventista* that brought together representatives of the radical Marxists as well as those *Vociani* who imagined that they spoke for what they considered the emerging Italian entrepreneurial class.

Mussolini was moved by all of this – particularly when Filippo Corridoni, a long time revolutionary and compatriot, joined the interventisti. More than that, once Italy entered the war against the Central Powers, Corridoni volunteered for combat. Before he left for the front – from which he was never to return – he wrote his final doctrinal piece, *Sindacalismo e Repubblica*, in which he argued that as a Marxist he understood the role of production in the nation's future. Together with his letters to comrades he made a case that the war would compel Italy to abandon its retrograde economy and undertake a commitment to rapid economic and industrial development. As a Marxist, he well understood the significance of industrial production in the nation's future. As a syndicalist he knew very well that Italy was at the precapitalist stage of economic development. In his judgment he was prepared to consider the possibility that the war might well serve as a catalyst that would stimulate self-sustained industrial growth on the peninsula.

Corridoni's piece appeared about the same time as that of Enrico Corradini's *La marcia dei produttori* –in which he heralded the appearance of a new entrepreneurial and industrializing element in Italy that would transform its future. At almost the same time, Prezzolini and Giovanni Papini published their *Vecchio e nuovo nazionalismo*. Together with the works of the radical syndicalists, Olivetti and Corridoni, the revolutionary ideology of a "New Italy" had begun to articulate itself. Like traditional Marxism, it emphasized *production* – the difference being that the new revolutionary syndicalism advocated the need to systematically increase production, while traditional Marxism expected economic maturity to have been obtained in the course of normal commodity production before the revolution. The syndicalists were advocates of revolutionary production; the orthodox Marxists were advocates of revolutionary distribution.

34

Traditional Marxism never advanced itself as an ideology of rapid economic development. Marxism expected its revolution to be post-industrial. In Italy, the ideology that was coming together with the advent of the Great War was one that expected to inspire rapid industrialization. Unlike traditional Marxism, the new national syndicalist ideology made the *nation* – rather than an international of the working class – the proper vehicle for its revolutionary purposes. A classless union of all citizens was its agent. In response to the coming together of all these doctrinal elements, Mussolini changed the subheading of his journal from "A Socialist Daily" to "A Daily of Producers and Combatants." He saw the future in the new ideology that had begun to draw itself together before the end of the Great War.

In the course of these developments, Mussolini made clear that he understood that the war made *production* an imperative necessity. The necessity of increased production for wartime and postwar Italy became a recurrent theme in all of his writings and speeches. The *nation* became the sustaining myth of his emerging revolution. In March 1919, the first meeting of the *Fasci di combattimento* was held in Milan and Mussolini articulated the principal elements of the transformative ideology that had emerged from the challenge of the Great War. At every critical point in the meeting in which Fascism was founded, Mussolini made reference to the centrality of the nation and the necessity of economic development for the achievement of revolutionary purpose. He believed that only through the revolutionary success of Fascism as he conceived it might Italy be restored to the first rank among modern nations.

Once the ideological motives that inspired Fascism are understood, much of its overt features can be appreciated. Because the peninsula was capital poor much of the supporting wealth necessary for the expansion of industry would have to be self-generated. The nation was called to obedience, sacrifice and intensified labor. The possessing classes, possessed of both wealth and entrepreneurial talent, were permitted to retain their position under increasingly close government supervision. Following the murder of Giacomo Matteotti in 1924 – which threatened the continuity of the Regime – Mussolini chose to impose dictatorial control over the nation's politics. What discipline and control were to mean became clear to everyone. The Fascist dictatorship became a reality. Both labor and capital became subject to central control. The government created vast enterprises of regulation – that ultimately shaped financial policy and the forms of development requisite to Fascism's conception of national needs. Wages and profits were subjected to various forms of control, with a Fascist bureaucracy becoming more and more dominant. Responding to enforced industrial peace, the first years of Fascist rule produced impressive growth in product as well as increasing sophistication in industry. The lack of natural resources impacted the process.

The first response to the lack of natural resources was the domestic effort to produce their surrogates. Hydroelectric power, for example, was developed as rapidly as possible. The nation's railroads were electrified. Time and motion studies were introduced to increase productivity without the employment of increased material inputs. Fascist labor organizations became conduits for government directives. Party representatives played the same role in the political control of industry. By the early 1930s, the Italian government controlled more of the nation's economy than was the case in any other European country with the obvious exception of the Soviet Union.

The distinction between the kinds of control imposed in Fascist Italy and those of the Soviet Union turned on the issue of the *ownership of property* – with Fascism allowing private ownership and the Soviets abolishing ownership in principle. The issue was more complex in terms of the *control of property*. While Fascism allowed private ownership, they rejected the liberal notion that individuals employed property to pursue their own interest. Fascists argued that the ownership of the means of production was a *social responsibility*. Ownership was seen, not as an opportunity for generating private profit, but as the best, immediate stimulant for rapid economic development.

Both the Fascist and Soviet systems were state-centered and party dominant. Neither allowed the existence of private property as it exists in traditional capitalist society. Fascists allowed private property, and the attendant existence of a basic market for the production and sale of commodities to survive. Their persistence allowed for incentives, more rational prices, and more balanced allocation of resources. Thus, by the mid-1920s, Mussolini was convinced that if Italy was to develop rapidly, allowing private ownership of property – duly controlled by state sponsored "corporativist" structures – would foster growth, provide a rational pricing policy for the economy, and allow for intersectoral balance. With some frequency, Mussolini spoke of an "Italian socialism" as the most humane and practical form of socialism for less developed nations in the twentieth century.

In effect, much of the overt features of Fascism could be understood as functions of Fascism's developmental ideology. That is the context in which Fascist social policy is to be understood. The introduction of some of the most advanced health and recreation programs for workers were all calculated to make Italy's work force more productive at least cost. To the same purpose the nation was provided cause for collective pride – with the highly visible national achievements in trans-Atlantic ocean and air crossings and international air-racing competitions. All of that contributed to the readiness to work, to sacrifice, and to conform to the strictures that characterized the new political dispensation.

To recognize that Fascism was a developmentally motivated authoritarianism is to provide the key to understanding its behavior. Its social policies become comprehensible. Its foreign policy begins to become comprehensible. The war in Ethiopia becomes a search for raw materials in an international environment already largely controlled by the "plutocratic" powers. Italian analysts spoke of Ethiopia's untapped resources. Together with that, a well established presence on the East coast of Africa promised Italy, as a growing trading nation, access to the trade routes outside the control of England's Suez passage. Fascist Italy's involvement in Spain – whatever its political motives – in part was inspired by a desire to reach the Atlantic without having to subject itself to British authority at Gibraltar. Italy was no longer to be "prisoner of the Mediterranean," traversing its own waters only at the sufferance of Great Britain.

All of this was contained in the Fascist doctrinal literature of the period. That Anglophone researchers chose not to read any of it made it necessary for them to devise their own "experimental names" to capture the "essence" of the Fascist phenomenon. They chose to see Fascism as incorrigibly "aggressive" in essence – neglecting to reflect on the armed expansion of the American and British empires through the precedent centuries.

More relevant to our purpose is the acknowledgment that the makers of Fascism did not conceal their political and social intentions. The makers of Fascism conceived themselves serving very specific purposes. The industrialization of their nation was an imperative. Much of their consequent behavior can be understood if we accept the realization that they behaved in a fashion shaped by the imperatives demanded by their convictions. The purpose here is not to justify Fascist behavior. It is to understand it. I am convinced that accepting their own characterization of their ideological imperatives allows us to more intelligently judge Fascism than any available alternative.[2]

---

[2]About the same time that my *The Ideology of Fascism* appeared, in which a case was advanced for Fascism's essentially developmental character, a similar study by Ludovico Garruccio, *L'industrializzazone tra nazionalismo e rivoluzione* made its appearance. We both followed an interpretive tradition that was part of non-Leninist Marxism during the interwar years. Before the Second World War, Arthur Rosenberg, as in independent Marxist theoretician, held that Fascism's "task" was to develop the retrograde economy of the Italian peninsula. In the early 1930s, Franz Borkenau argued that with the end of the Great War what Italy required was not Marxist-Leninist revolution but a radical increase in overall national productivity. That was the sense in which Fascism was to be understood. In fact, after the Second World War,

The purposes of experimental naming are *heuristic* – suggestive of further research. Understanding the ideology of Fascism as committed to rapid economic, specifically industrial, development suggests a great deal about its population control, its political institutions, and its domestic and foreign policies. Compared to its alternatives, understanding Fascism as a movement having rapid industrialization as its primary objective allows us to anticipate a great deal about its conduct.

In your research on Fascism you have suggested that in order to fully understand the Regime it is important to consider it in the context of "dictatorships of development." You argue that Fascism promoted the rapid economic development of the peninsula through the forced accumulation of capital and the politics of modernization – to produce an industrial sector that proved capable of supporting the nation's postwar economic boom. The work in which you made your case – "Italian Fascism and Developmental Dictatorship" was sufficiently well received to merit its recent reissuance by Princeton University Press Legacy Library. Nonetheless, in your own country, there have been criticisms levelled against your thesis. How would you explain that?

Any historical or sociological work that attempts to interpret large scale phenomena is invariably open to criticism. The reasons for that are not far to seek. Social science

---

that is precisely how Mihali Vajda, a researcher in the Hungarian Academy of Science in Budapest, conceived Italian Fascism. It was a revolutionary movement responding to the manifest needs of a retrograde economy. It intended to rapidly industrialize the nation – and was so to be understood.

propositions are generally *discursive* rather than *quantitative* – and when the research involves entire epochs, the discussion is conducted using informal logic and plausibilities. That provides ample opportunity for criticism – warranted or not. While researchers welcome quantitative data, such data is usually of supplementary importance. The main thrust of the discussion is generally conducted in ordinary language. Social science is not physics or chemistry. At best, social science offers evidenced plausibilities. Thus any account of Fascism's developmental efforts uses funded data, collected by one or another agency, to make its case. In the work mentioned, dealing with Fascism's developmental efforts, I employed data collected after the Second World War by the Twentieth Century Fund – at a time, presumably, when there was little, if any, reason to lie through omission or distortion. That data showed Fascist Italy among the most, if not the most, rapidly growing economies in Europe. Could such data be questioned? Of course. Economic statistics are among the most difficult data to collect and interpret. There are an indeterminate number of reasons why one must be cautious with data. Even the most credible data, if employed in dealing with a highly charged political issue, predictably will become subject to objections. In such a climate, we can fully expect someone to take exception to the most carefully collected and represented statistics. Deciding who is correct in such circumstances is very difficult to establish. If the environment is one permeated by a strongly held political sentiment, one can expect criticisms – whether such criticisms are merited or not. In the Anglophone community, the term "fascism" is a universal term of abuse. To use the term, or to discuss the political system in which it originated, with anything other than repugnance, is to court public rejection. (One critic of my work pointedly asked if I had "forgotten the death of six million innocent Jews?")

While there are criticisms of my work that are perfectly legitimate (I will deal with some in the course of these conversations), many are not. Some take issue with the characterization of Italian Fascism as a rational response to the crisis of economic retardation and its exacerbation in the Great War. They cite cases in which Fascism undertook policies that were "anti-economic" – like the insistence on the "quota novanta" in the question of the exchange rate for Italy's lire – or in terms of its policy of "autarchy." Such individual policies may well have had dysfunctional effect. They may have well militated against the nation's economic health. However correct such judgments might be, they do not render the general policy of the Regime economically irrational. Such policies may well have been determined by political, rather than economic, rationality. The issue of national pride and all its attendant sentiments may have prompted the effort to maintain a given currency exchange rate against the pound sterling. Reasonable fear that its enemies might embargo essential resources at critical times would recommend a policy of autarchy. Such episodic policies might well negatively impact strictly economic concerns – but that would not render Fascist Italy any less a developmental dictatorship. It would be a developmental dictatorship responding to noneconomic, but critical, concerns. The question then arises, how many times might the Fascist government undertake policies that would negatively impact the economy before it could be classified as antidevelopmental in character?

It is almost impossible to provide a brief and convincing response to such specific questions about Fascist economic policy. First, it must be understood that periods of relative autarchy, for example, characterize almost every developmental system – prompted by international circumstances, national peculiarities, as well as the relative stage of growth. If we consider only the mass-mobilizing, reactive nationalist, party dominant and state-centered systems, we find that they all, for different reasons, went through similar periods. Lenin, for his own reasons, opened post-revolutionary Russia to the international economy. Stalin, in turn, imposed a program of relatively autonomous development (i.e., autarchy) on the nation. Mao Zedong attempted autonomous development (with the exception of economic traffic with the Soviet Union). Deng Xiaoping specifically objected to Mao's "autarchic" policies and opened China to foreign capital and foreign commerce. Stalin's policies imposed enormous cost on the Soviet population – including the exploitation of labor and the death of millions. Mao's essentially autarchic policies similarly imposed a degree of exploitation and death on China never before recorded in its history. Both Stalin and Mao conceived the period of relative autarchy as one in which investment capital for industrial growth would be extracted from the general population. For his part, Marx spoke of such a process as the "stage of primitive capital accumulation," and identified it as part of the process of economic maturation that was to have concluded long before the socialist revolution. That suggests something about all systems of rapid growth and technological change. It is particularly relevant to systems of late development.

It is in that comparative context that the brief attempt at unsystematic and poorly applied autarchic experiments in Fascist Italy must be considered. Its costs were high and its results relatively meager – but nowhere near the costs exacted from the Russian, Chinese, North Korean, or Cambodian people by their regimes during a similar period.

In Fascist Italy, other than the fact that episodes of indigenous development are part of the general pattern of economic policies, they were shaped by peculiar factors operating in the world of the 1930s. Fascist strategists regularly argued that Italy was singularly resource poor. That made it particularly vulnerable to the whimsy of the "plutocracies." Without some change in its circumstances, Italy would be forever hostage to foreign sources for essential raw materials. Sanctions, at any time, could deny the nation its most fundamental needs. For that reason, it was argued that the nation required substitutes for critical components of its economy – and provision for its armed forces. Ultimately, the fateful argument was made that Abyssinia would supply just those critical resources.

In any event, whatever motivated the poorly contrived policy of autarchy in Fascist Italy, it certainly did not last long, nor was it part of a plan to exploit Italian labor for the special benefit of capitalists, or to retard economic growth – any more than it was part of the plan of Stalin, Mao, Kim Il Sung, or Pol Pot, to cause the unnatural death of millions of their citizens. What can be said is that Fascist autarchy cost Italians far less than analogous programs cost Russians, Chinese North Koreans, or Cambodians. Moreover, the brief autarchic phase of Italian development certainly cost less than the long and grueling "primitive capital accumulation" that we find documented in the history of the Anglo-Saxon industrial revolution. One need only remember the exploitation of labor – of women, children, and of slavery – not to speak of the entire issue of colonization/imperialism.

None of these issues can be definitively resolved. Whatever answers are tendered, they rarely satisfy. These kinds of issues are joined largely to serve polemical purpose. Rarely are they introduced for cognitive enlightenment. They are generally framed in such a fashion as to question the moral integrity of any author who does not insist upon the essential malevolence of "fascism."

Such sentiments give rise to questions that can never be satisfactorily answered. They arise amid that company that has deemed "fascism" (usually meaning Hitler's National Socialism) to be intrinsically, and irrevocably immoral. The entire company wishes only to read accounts that condemn everything about the Regime and its agents. Such versions enjoy credibility – because they exploit the accounts of the costs of Fascism to the people of Italy, as well as to the United State and Europe in their entirety. While such accounts are emotionally arresting, they really tell us very little about the political system that is the object of attention.

One can write an account of the political history of the Soviet Union as rich in invectives and outrage as any devoted to "fascism." It would be of as little help as a great deal of the literature produced after the Second World War devoted to exposing the "essence of fascism." Unhappily, no less can be said of similar accounts of the Chinese system under Mao Zedong, and the monstrous system we now associate with

Pol Pot. But more than that, it is well to remember that left-wing intellectuals have managed to put together similar lamentations about the "immoral essence of capitalism" in general, and of "imperialism" in particular. None of this is particularly helpful in attempting to understand any of them.

Clearly, all social science accounts of complex phenomena are subject to legitimate criticism. In general legitimate criticism furthers the work of social science. That is why "project terms" are introduced – to orient inquiry and stimulate increasing precision – as well as prompt meaningful questions. Sustained bias and prevailing prejudgment militates against serious social science inquiry. Only with the appropriate objectivity might one inquire into the kinds of questions that further inquiry

In your exposition you have raised another issue that has engaged the interests of many. It turns on the anti-materialistic revision of Marxism undertaken by Mussolini and Olivetti. Zeev Sternhell, the Israeli academician, has emphasized that particular aspect of the revision to the point where he has argued that the ideology of Fascism developed in France out of the confluence of the socialism of Sorel and the nationalism of Maurras. Do you share such a notion of the French origins of Fascism?

A great many scholars who began to take Fascist ideology seriously in the 1960s alluded to the complex set of influences that contributed to the making of the system of beliefs that brought Mussolini to power in 1922. Because Sternhell's work was so impressive – objective and intelligently crafted – his judgments exercised significant impact on the academic community. There clearly were French elements in the ideology of Fascism – but there also were German and Austrian constituents as well. In its final form, the ideology of Fascism was unique, neither identical with nor replicated by any other political system.

That is only to be expected – and neither Sternhell nor any other commentator meant anything more. Serious research has made several things reasonably clear. Marxism, in its original Germanic form, arrived in France considerably modified by English influence. One need only compare Marx's *The Holy Family* with his essays written after his long sojourn in England. Marxism, whatever the form in which it arrived in France, had very little immediate impact on revolutionary thought. Marx spent two decades after the publication of the first volume of *Das Kapital* trying to make Frenchmen into Marxists who believed that the entirety of the world's material and psychological conduct was governed exclusively by "natural laws" that operated independently of human will and resolve.

It took a great deal of time and effort to convince the French, however revolutionary, to lend credence to any of that. Many remained resolutely Proudhonists, followers of Pierre-Jean Proudhon, who, while he insisted that revolutions "spring out of the necessity of things," qualified that by maintaining that revolutions were "acts of sovereign justice, in the order of moral facts." On more than one occasion he spoke of the failure of revolution because of a "total lack of ideas." Even after his death, French revolutionaries conceived radical political change a function of moral conviction and the availability of ideas capable of engaging the sentiment of "masses." Even as Marxism became increasingly prominent, there were many Frenchmen who continued to see revolution in terms of moral conflict, heroic commitment, and personal sacrifice. Georges Sorel became their spokesman. He always thought of politics in terms of the virtues of antiquity, in terms of moral challenges, mortal risk, sacrificial dedication, and heroic gesture. Sorel imagined revolution as the marshaling of masses – employing sign and symbol in the fashion described in the work of Gustave Le Bon.

Sorel saw revolution as the business of inspired men and engaged masses – not the epiphenomena of economic affairs. The collection of revolutionaries most inspired by such anti-materialist ideas were syndicalists. They were iconoclasts, influenced by Sorel's dynamic sense of purpose. In the course of anticipating their evolution, they had come to appreciate the fact that orthodox Marxism had very little to offer. Classical Marxism spoke of an inevitable revolution that would engulf communities sinking under the weight of over-production – communities whose economies could not profit by the clearing of inventory; communities condemned to catastrophic collapse.

Because of classical Marxism's peculiar over-productionist/under-consumptionist economic theory, it argued that social revolution was positively correlated with the increasing maturity of a community's productive base. Conversely, the less developed the economy of any given community, the less revolutionary potential. According to an ordinary interpretation of the theory, England would be ready for revolution before France. It was reasonably clear that there were significant numbers of French revolutionaries who balked at such a notion.

All these ideas found eager acceptance in Italy. As soon as Sorel's writings were introduced into the peninsula, a collection of aggressive, capable, and assertive intellectuals were ready to identify themselves as "syndicalists." Together with gifted social scientists like Sergio Panunzio, and talented economists of the stature of Arturo Labriola, they were prepared to consider all viable social and philosophical ideas. Their citations, among others, included references to Ludwig Gumplowicz, Gaetano Mosca, Vilfredo Pareto, and Maffeo Pantaleoni. They were less concerned with orthodoxy than with solutions. As a consequence, by the time syndicalism had taken first root in Italy, it had assumed its own particular features. Some of the first articles of A. O. Olivetti in his *Pagine libere* spoke a language other than that of orthodox Marxism. As early as 1907, he affirmed that "no one any longer" believed in a revolution that was the inevitable result of some set of arcane "laws" – that operated independent of the will and passion of human beings. He was to talk of a "new Marxism," that was destined to move human beings to action – part of its inspiration arising out of an abiding sense of humiliation that afflicted Italians – the result of its protracted interaction with nations that were economically more advanced. Italy had failed to achieve even the most basic industrialization and was reduced to beggary – forcing its citizens to emigrate in the effort to survive, and selling its heritage to tourists for a pittance. It was disadvantaged by the conditions governing international finance and international trade. In all of that there was an unmistakable sense of frustrated nationalism that was to regularly surface in Olivetti's prose. (At almost the same time, Michels, already a syndicalist, maintained that nationalism was a heartfelt sentiment that would have to be accommodated in the forthcoming "internationalist" revolution.)

The fact is that years before the Great War, syndicalism was more than a Marxism – it had been substantially modified. It included an emphasis on will and conscious resolve. It included nationalism and an acknowledgment of economic backwardness. Nonetheless, in the essays by syndicalists, there remained ample room for anti-bourgeois, and anti-state sentiment, together with an insistence on violent class conflict. In its advocacy there were unmistakable elements of Sorelianism and Proudhonism. Still, there was something other than that. Syndicalism in Italy had become increasingly Italian. By the coming of the Great War, the anti-statism, and the emphasis on class warfare, had been moderated – perhaps by the influence of the "New Nationalism" of the followers of Enrico Corradini (and Prezzolini and Papini). By 1913, the democratic nationalists had left the Nationalist Association, and it had attracted authoritarian nationalists like Alfredo Rocco into its ranks. He brought with him the ideas of Friedrich List – a principled opponent of Karl Marx and a proponent of rapid national economic development.

Rocco was an advocate of state intervention in the nation's economy – particularly that nation prepared to, or that had embarked upon, a drive to industrial maturity. He emphasized a view of a community's economy radically different from that of the founders of Marxism. Rocco was a *productionist* – rather than an *over-productionist*. He anticipated a union of the state with politically organized labor and enterprise in a program of economic modernization.

Engels had spoken of the "withering away of the state" at the conclusion of the anticipated social revolution – while Rocco, and the nationalists of Corradini, together with an increasing number of syndicalists, conceived the state as an active, and perhaps determinative, actor in a nation's rapid economic modernization and industrialization.

Thus, even before the Great War, Italian syndicalism distinguished itself from that of France. Whatever influence Maurras was to have on the evolution of Fascist thought, it was secondary to the confluence of ideas originating among Italian nationalists and syndicalists. While the Great War forced nationalist and developmental ideas on the revolutionary leadership of the peninsula, the outlines of a *national syndicalism* were already apparent. Syndicalists began to moderate their objections to the state – and began to appeal to a set of common interests that united all members of the nation in a community of destiny. Thus, although originally inspired by French ideas, *developmental nationalism* was to substantively influence the thought of Italy's radical intellectuals before the coming of the Great War. In so doing, developmental nationalism made of syndicalism an essentially Italian product.

As has been indicated, by the time of the War in Tripoli, Olivetti had suggested an affinity between revolutionary syndicalism and developmental nationalism. Having made the allusion, a flood of "unorthodox" ideas influenced the changing substance of Italian syndicalism – to render it increasingly Italian. There was interaction with Prezzolini and the *Vociani*, who spoke of the backwardness of the nation's economic base, and the critical need for rapid development. Prezzolini had written an account of syndicalism in 1909 in which he spoke of the community of interests between the proletariat and the bourgeoisie of the peninsula. He spoke of that as the intellectual basis for an Italian nationalism that would unite all members of the community in a common enterprise. Prezzolini, and those he influenced, appealed to the somnolent virtues of masses; he spoke of revolutionaries who would awaken the dormant qualities that had made Italy, more than once, a leader among nations and the creator of civilizations.

Before the Great War, Mussolini was only an uncommitted and casual participant of all this. He wrote articles about Olivetti, and he reviewed Prezzolini's book on syndicalism. His work was essentially noncommittal, but it was evident that he was informed about developments. While he worked in Austria-Hungary as a socialist organizer, he sometimes found occasion to employ syndicalist ideas in the service of the resident Italian minority. With some qualification, however, he remained an "orthodox" Marxist. He expected to rise in the ranks of the Socialist party, and to drift too far afield from official doctrine would have impaired his career goals.

That did not preclude substantial correspondence with Prezzolini nor admiration for some of the positions entertained by syndicalist theoreticians. Mussolini possessed an active intelligence – and he wrote abundantly for the socialist press. He wrote reviews of works by syndicalists (such as Michels) as well as those by "bourgeois" specialists (Pareto, for example), and Russian expatriates (like Petr Kropotkin, for example), and while his public image was that of an orthodox Marxist, it was clear that Mussolini was becoming increasingly restive, confined as he was by a Party definition of "orthodoxy." Before the war actually took shape on the horizon, he founded his own journal, free of Party supervision, entitled *Utopia*, which regularly published works by syndicalists and syndicalist sympathizers. It was a journal whose content allows us to judge how far Mussolini was prepared to depart from the orthodoxy of Party discipline.

Whatever the case, it was clear by the time of the coming of the Great War, Italian syndicalism had forged a belief system that explicitly appealed to nationalism – a *national syndicalism* – unmatched in range of thought and implications – only later to share features with the syndicalism of other countries and cultures. Years later, in 1930, Olivetti wrote his account of Italian syndicalism's development from the initial impulse that originated with Sorel, until it came to provide something of the belief system of Fascism (*Lineamenti del nuovo stato italiano*). At that juncture, and in retrospect, Olivetti insisted that Italian syndicalism, that found its origins in Sorel, had soon formulated a set of original concepts that anticipated a new form of nationalism that would find material expression in an "ordered society of producers" under the auspices of a unitarian state that expressed the will of a people prepared to meet the existential challenges of the twentieth century. In his judgment, a singularly Italian syndicalism had provided some of the critical components of what had become Fascism.

In the context of these developments, what was the contribution of Giovanni Gentile to the revision of Marxism and the articulation of Fascism's ideology?

Until and through the Great War, Gentile largely pursued his own professional interests, completing the academic work

53

that occupied him. He did, however, take the occasion, in 1897-99, the write and publish two studies on the Marxism of Karl Marx and Friedrich Engels. Stimulated by discussions with Benedetto Croce, he addressed the entire issue of the interpretation of classical Marxism as a theory of history and a general system of philosophy.

As it turned out, in dealing with Marxism as a theory of history, the young Gentile expanded on the criticism that had already found expression among the syndicalists. He was to give the criticism explicit form, in the course of which he laid down some of the founding principles of the belief system of Fascism.

Years later, in retrospect, Gentile fully appreciated what he had done. During the years of Fascism's full maturity, Gentile was to affirm that he had been a "fascist" long before there was a Fascism. He took it upon himself to insert in the later editions of his *Discorsi di religione* the claim that he had been a Fascist since 1875 – from the moment of his conscious existence! While hyperbolic in expression, the claim was meant to signify that the least awareness of a conscious existence carried implications that led to his formal philosophy – and his formal philosophy led irresistibly to Fascism.

For his entire life as an intellectual, Gentile was convinced that his philosophy provided the cognitive foundation for the doctrine of Fascism. Gentile argued that every, and any, political movement, however reticent to proclaim a foundation in philosophy, nonetheless invariably rooted its conduct in at least the semblance of thought systematically pursued. For Gentile, action bespoke thought. Thought that did not manifest itself in action was velleity. Conversely, Gentile recognized that there was action that did not engage serious thought – and, as such, to be dismissed as completely devoid of cognitive or moral substance.

When, in his youth, he discussed Marxism, he argued that Marx really had never settled upon a serious *metaphysics* for his political practice. When Engels, in his maturity, maintained that Marxism was a "dialectical materialism" – he sought to supply that missing foundation. Gentile was to argue that the materialism contained in the writings of Engels was conceptually flawed and that Marx was sophisticated enough to recognize its deficiencies. Marx never associated his belief system with "dialectical materialism." In effect, rather than associate his system with the crude metaphysics of Engels' materialism, he preferred to leave his Marxism without a credible substructure. In Gentile's judgment, whatever "materialism" Marx had made his own, was really an empiricism made to serve as a metaphysics, lacking depth, and belied by his earlier writings. In his critique of Ludwig Feuerbach, Marx spoke unselfconsciously of a "materialism" that displayed all the properties of "spirit." Although he never developed these early insights, it was clear that whatever materialism Marx harbored, it certainly was not the dialectical materialism of Engels.

For Gentile, Marx never provided the philosophical (metaphysical) foundation for his political beliefs. His followers had simply proceeded with the political program (presumably embodied in the *Communist Manifesto*) – without the support of an argued philosophical base. Since that kind of Marxism was simply a collection of empirical claims about economic society, every empirical change in the collection altered the belief system. The result was a system that was in constant modification – and that, by the turn of the twentieth century, had given rise to more than a dozen competitive variants.

Gentile's concern with the philosophical, essentially metaphysical, foundations of a political system of beliefs, was (at least in part) the consequence of his conviction that materialism, and the empiricism it implied, rendered human beings passive in the face of external reality. Materialism implied that human beings, as sentient creatures, were reactive subjects, responding to sensory inputs, to external stimuli, in order to act. Gentile argued that human beings were not the subjects of external forces, but the *initiators* of action, directors of their own destiny. Moved by principle, sentiment, and anticipations of the future, human beings made history, rather than being its objects.

By the time of the coming of the Great War, Gentile already was a recognized figure among Italian intellectuals. The central themes of his thought were already known among the best informed. When Mussolini, already restless with the rising international tension that would lead to war, chose to found his own journal, *Utopia*, its content reveals a great deal about the association of Gentile's Actualism and Mussolini's evolving beliefs. Mussolini founded *Utopia* in order to explore political ideas free of the constraints of Marxist orthodoxy, as the Socialist Party understood that orthodoxy. He wished to pursue answers to the questions that had collected around the socialism of which he was spokesman. In the course of that, the material published in the pages of his journal reveals a great deal about the association of Gentile's Actualism and Mussolini's political beliefs.

In the pages of *Utopia* one finds references to Gentile's ideas, citation of his works, and an implied criticism of the orthodoxy that had collected around institutional Marxism. There were a number of reasonably prominent Italian thinkers who saw Gentile's emphasis on the spiritual elements in the evolving history of humanity as critical to the needs of society. Particularly notable was a long essay by Panunzio, already established as a prominent theoretician of Italian syndicalism. He specifically made the case for human initiative, moral judgments, determination, and resolute commitment, in the making of national history – all in language made familiar by Gentile. In that turbulent time, that marked the beginning of Mussolini's break with orthodox socialism, Gentile's influence was apparent, and in retrospect, influential.

Gentile continued to comment on the war. His associations were primarily with the developmental nationalists of the period. He published several articles for nationalist publications – and expressed clear concern for Italy's economic, and particularly industrial, development. He spoke of a "New Italy," peopled by "New Italians." It would be an Italy that would leave behind all the problematic traits of the old Italy. It would be spirited and self-motivated, united and community oriented.

By the time the Great War concluded, Pippo Corridoni had died a martyr for the revolution that all syndicalists conceived as imminent. Like Olivetti, he had understood that developmental nationalism would be at the center of revolutionary fulfillment. They all spoke of spiritual energy, the felt commitment to the creation of a Greater Italy. Gentile's Actualism provided the philosophical substructure for all of that. When Mussolini arose, in March 1919, to gather followers around the standards of the *Fasci di combattimento*, he expressed the beliefs that were expected to inspire those who had sacrificed for the victory of the nation. It was a system of beliefs that contained those elements provided by the emergent national syndicalism, features found in the developmental nationalism of Corradini's Blueshirts, together with the political theater of Marinetti's Futurists. Gentile's contribution was implicit. It was the rationale for the commitment that (at least temporarily) united them all.

After the March on Rome, Gentile was no longer reserved. In 1923, he joined the *Partito nazionale fascista*. It was at that time, in response to queries from Party comrades, that Mussolini spoke, without reservations, of Gentile as his "teacher." Thereafter, Gentile became the spokesman for the Party's political, philosophical, and metaphysical beliefs. When the formal *Dottrina del fascismo* appeared in 1932, the philosophical portion was the work of Gentile. Signed by Mussolini, it became the official statement of Fascism's rationale. Today, there are few serious scholars who do not acknowledge the contribution of Gentile to the intellectual evolution of Fascism. Until the mid-1930s, there could be no question of Gentile's role in the public defense, and the increasingly sophisticated depiction of Fascism's corporative state.

Even as he became increasingly alienated from the Regime as a result of its increasing rapprochement with Hitler's Germany – and the imposition of special "racial laws" – he made no public criticism. His beliefs did not allow him that. He believed resistance to the errors of the Regime would have to be conducted from within the system. To have done otherwise, in his judgment, would have been a betrayal of the principles he had taught all his life. In his personal life he sought to defend Jews as well as citizens who had done nothing more than object to some feature of Fascism. He was assassinated on his return from an effort to defend anti-fascist intellectuals at a local university.

Recently, Fabio Farotti, in his *Gentile e Mussolini*, has restated the case for acknowledging that Gentile was the philosopher of Fascism – to which I would have little to add. When, at the end of his life, Gentile wrote a final statement of his social and political philosophy in his *Genesi e struttura della società* – it was a rationale for the ideal Fascist society. Gentile not only lived and died a Fascist, his life work provided the philosophical basis for the system.

In what explicit sense do you understand Gentile's Actualism provided the philosophic foundation for the Fascist state?

That Giovanni Gentile provided Fascist with its "logic," its "conscience," and its "justification" turns on the character of his epistemology (and perhaps his metaphysics). Gentile was convinced that reality displayed all the properties of mind, spirit, and/or consciousness: choice, rationality, liberty. He believed that we, as a community and as individuals, were (in some ultimate sense) responsible for the world. He saw it as our creation. (He was an immanentist – we are not in the world, the world is in us.) He opposed the notion that we find ourselves in a finished, "external" world – with material objects opposing us. Instead, he argued that the world was a product of our collective and individual consciousness. We constructed realty by accepting or rejecting what we have been taught (beginning with the rules of evidence, for example). We were once taught that the earth was flat, and we accepted that. We now hold it to be a sphere – with the same confidence (in part because we have largely accepted strictly *scientific* rules of evidence). We talk of "discovering" the external world – but we do not "discover" it as explorers discover things. We accept or reject things we have learned – the criteria of truth, for example – through a conscious decision, an active act of will – and thereby *shape* the world and everything in it. In effect, we are ultimately responsible for the world we live in. (Rather than try to deliver Gentile's basic philosophy in a few sentences, I suggest readers read Gentile's *Teoria generale dello spirito come atto puro.*) That kind of understanding of the world and how we function in it, makes us, individually and collectively, responsible. We live in an intensely moral universe. We are to be responsible, dedicated, and prepared to sacrifice for the creation of a world that satisfies our moral sensibilities. The fundamental issue is, what kind of world would we like to create for ourselves and our children? Gentile gives us some guidance in the articles he wrote at the end of the Great War. (See, for example, "Dopo la vittoria," and some of the articles he wrote for the Nationalist press right after the end of the war.) Once we accept our responsibilities we commit ourselves to labor and the discharge of our obligations. For Gentile, the responsibility of citizens is to work for the restoration of the grandeur of their community – for that would be part of the process of fulfilling ourselves. His vision of a future Italy was one that transcended the present – the "Italietta" of his time. It would be an Italy that would shed the sense of inferiority that resulted from the humiliations inflicted upon it by the "Great Powers." He saw his future Italy as a powerful nation – exceptional in its prospects – a "Third Rome," peopled by a "New Humanity," educated to moral obligations. The Italy he anticipated would be an industrialized Italy, capable of projecting its power. To accomplish all that, Italians would have to be prepared to sacrifice, to labor, and to commit themselves. All of that follows from the conviction that we are responsible for the world we live in – and which we will leave to our children. Gentile saw education as the major tool in the transformation of Italians (see his *La reforma dell'educazone*). He made all this prominent *before* the advent of Fascism. He was, in effect, a Fascist before there was Fascism.

Because he was an immanentist, Gentile conceived society not as something constructed by and external to humanity, but as something immanent – as *interiore homine*. We are not in society, society is in us. Once understood, we appreciate that we and society are *one* – we are a "totality" – the true nature of humanity is *totalitarian*. We learn from each other; if our plans are not empty expressions, we must work together; we must create a union of intent; we must transcend differences. We must create a seamless union. That would be accomplished through patient, but stern education. (See the entire discussion in *Genesi e struttura della società*.) Such a totalitarian community – in which the community and the individual are one – can find its voice in a single human being (what Roberto Michels called a "charismatic"). Gentile saw the individual and the state as one – a union of beliefs, sentiments, and aspirations – that can find its voice in one leader.

61

Granted that, what was the role of other intellectuals – such as Prezzolini, Michels, and Panunzio – in the entire drama? Would you agree that Fascism – more than anything else – was a cultural revolution, a revolution in how one might think about the world?

These are both difficult questions to answer with brevity. The second really has no objective answer. It is clearly a matter of judgment. The first question has an answer, but is not directly related to the answer to the second.

Prezzolini has always been a very popular essayist in Italy. This was particularly true before, and during the Great War. He synthesized broad currents of opinion. He wrote insightful works on pragmatism, syndicalism, and national industrial development. He was in many ways more gifted than the average intellectual. He awakened many to questions that were critical to the future of Italy in the twentieth century. He could write, with conviction, about popular belief systems that colored popular opinion. We know that he influenced Mussolini when Mussolini was searching for a rational perspective on Italian radical politics. The opinions of Prezzolini did influence Mussolini, particularly during the decade before the Great War. More than that, we have every evidence that Prezzolini's views influenced educated Italians to the challenges that the nation faced, and would face, in the immediate future. Prezzolini worked with, and respected, Gentile – and was familiar with his basic philosophical opinions – communicating them to a national audience at the most critical times in Italy's history. Acknowledging that, it was true that Prezzolini was constitutionally incapable of simply being a Fascist. He would always be critical. That is who he was. When I knew him, he was still critical, but objective, and fair in his judgment of people and events. He was more knowledgeable about Fascism than most of my academic colleagues.

Michels, as a revolutionary syndicalist, provided Fascist revolutionaries with what became their standard arguments against representative democracy, in general, and parliamentary systems, in particular. He did not pretend to be a philosopher. He was an empirical social scientist – and his publications on Fascism remain among the best studies of the system. For example, he applied the insights of Le Bon and Sorel to the Fascist experience. He brought the work of Italian sociologists into the stream of Fascist reflections. Beyond Italy (his adopted homeland), his thought was seminal in the founding of sociology as an internationally recognized empirical discipline. Fascist thought would have been diminished by his absence. When he died, the PNF identified him as a "departed comrade."

Among those who contributed to the intellectual substance of Fascism, Panunzio played a distinctive role. He was not a philosopher, although some of his commentaries on modern philosophy remain remarkably intuitive. Panunzio's most fundamental interest was jurisprudence and institutional applications. His published works either anticipate or reflect developments of Fascism, first as a mass mobilizing revolution, and then as a growing set of institutions that were to result in the "Corporative State." As a syndicalist, he gave expression to the form of revolutionary Marxism that was to produce the first Fascism. His *Teoria generale dello stato fascista* remains among the best single works on the cognitive foundation and the institutional character of the Fascist State. Even the rare Anglophone scholars who have chosen to read the ideological literature of Fascism have credited him with being one of the two most important intellectual architects of Fascism.

Each of the intellectuals you have cited was important in the sequence of events that transformed Italy from 1922 until the catastrophe of the Second World War. Each contributed to that sequence in his own fashion. All were important in that sequence for different reasons – but each was important. Without any one of them, Fascism would have been perceptibly different.

All of which brings us to that question for which there is no convincing answer. What was Fascism? I cannot pretend to answer so broad and all-encompassing question. Fascism was no one thing. It was a complex product of so many confluent influences – so unique that we will never see its like again. Like all historical events, it is idiographic, a uniqueness in time and space. Containing elements that share a family resemblance with others experienced elsewhere and in different times – it nonetheless remains unique unto itself.

If one reflects on Italy at the time of the coming of Fascism, one can begin to address the question of what it may have been. Fascism came to a nation that had just won victory in the most destructive war in history. Six hundred thousand young Italians had paid for the victory with their lives. Many more returned home forever maimed and disfigured. But the young Italians had stood fast at the Piave – against the best the Austrians and Germans could throw against them. In returning home, they found themselves threatened and insulted by the organized socialists who had opposed the war. Demeaned as "lackies" and "janissaries" of the "capitalists," denied public services by socialist labor unions, and on more than one occasion, assaulted and brutalized by Marxist opponents, the veterans, who had fought so long at so great a cost, were prepared to respond. After socialist radicals had seized the factories, and the government in Rome held it more prudent not to attempt to dislodge them, veteran groups began to come together – to oppose their tormentors. They came together to destroy the entire infrastructure of socialist political organization and agitation. Fascism, newly organized, became their institutional base, their rallying centers, and frequently, their major financial resource.

It was evident to anyone with political acumen that the millions of war veterans constituted a demographic that could serve political purpose. The traditional parties, as well as the post-war parties that collected around the Roman Catholics and the socialists, exploited them as a population resource. The Fascists, however, were specially favored. They clearly addressed the dominant sentiments that moved the veterans as a group. Fascists celebrated sacrifice and exalted patriotism; they saw, in the sacrifice of an entire generation, in their selfless response to the call of duty, the making of a new nation – more powerful, more respected, and the bearer of more responsibilities, than the old.

The developmental and modernizing nationalists, the Futurists, and the national syndicalists, all gathering around – to provide intellectual content and political theater to a movement that expanded exponentially, until there was a Fascist organization in every city, town, and hamlet on the peninsula. Identified with a doctrine that promised an economic program that would offer opportunities for all, urban and rural, worker and capitalist alike, Fascism's momentum was irresistible.

By 1921, the organized socialists had succeeded in alienating the enterprisory class, the agriculturists, the domestic security forces, a significant portion of the working class, and the members of the armed forces, ranging from the members of the general staff to the lowliest foot-soldier who had survived the carnage of the war. As an inescapable consequence, by that time, there was not a single, organized, political force on the peninsula that could resist the Fascist demand for a leadership position in Rome. .

Making Italy a "Great Nation" was the mobilizing myth of the Fascist movement. It drew its strength from the veteran groups and the rising producer class – the "emergent bourgeoisie" – to which De Felice made ready reference. Passive support came from all those groups that had reason to fear "Bolshevik revolution." The newly arisen Leninists among the socialists had frightened everyone who had the most meager property to defend. In addition to that, they offended nationalists of all, and any, sort.

What held all these population elements together was an ideology and a doctrine that offered each a material or psychological benefit. Italy was to become a great productive community that would assure not only profitable enterprise and labor opportunities – but the satisfaction of being a member of a rising power, a Great Nation. The old community of mandolin players and tour guides, would disappear into history. In its place would arise an assembly of culture creators, a community that would write a memorable history – commensurate with the sacrifice of all the youthful dead who had made that future possible. It would be a New Italy animated by the heroic virtues that had carried the old Italy to victory at Vittorio Veneto. All those virtues that had given color to the syndicalism of Sorel became more than philosophical accompaniments to social revolution. The war had made those virtues singularly functional. They had been instilled in the ranks of ordinary soldiers who marched forward to die in the trenches – in order that others would forge on to victory. It was not Sorel, or Henri Bergson, or Friedrich Nietzsche who made those ideas viable. Without the post-war circumstances and without those political thinkers like Corridoni, Marinetti, Corradini, Rocco, Panunzio, and a number of others, the moral virtues so much recommended by Sorel would have remained peripheral to events. The political genius of Fascism was its ability to pull together all the strands of revolutionary opinion that had made their appearance before and during the time of the Great War – and enlist them in the service of a national program of economic growth and industrial development. It was presented, in its virtual entirety during the meeting that saw the founding of Fascism.

Certainly Fascism was a cultural revolution. It was a revolution in thought. But it was not only that. It was a program for the nation's uplift. As such, that is what made its advocacy of a "transformation of values" so important. That is what made the moral and cognitive revolution meaningful. Today, the most eloquent among us, can preach those same virtues anywhere in the West – and those ideas would be nothing more than an object of derision and/or indifference. The ideas, no matter how laudable, would have remained curiosities independent of the circumstances that attended the social environment of Italy after the Great War.

Was Fascism, then, simply a response on the part of a "proletarian" nation intending to achieve the status of a Great Power – opposing itself to the impostures of the prevailing "plutocracies" – or was it, above all else, a general ideological reaction to the demo-liberal system?

I would argue that it was something of both. Clearly, the first Fascists were committed to making of their Italy a "great power" – a competitor of the advanced powers that had established military, economic, and cultural sway over the remainder of the community of nations. The industrially more advanced powers exercised control over about eighty percent of the inhabited earth. They controlled passage on the seas. They arbitrarily established the boundaries of communities that had adequately maintained their own arrangements from time immemorial. They regularly demeaned the lesser communities; they deplored their collective behavior, dismissed their creativity, faulted their judgments, and obstructed their aspirations. The advanced powers further diminished the historical significance of those they found less powerful by arguing that even though enjoying a history of achievement and distinction they had corrupted their talents by recurrent intermixture with lesser people. Italy was considered to be among such "spoiled" peoples.

The first Fascists were animated by the conviction that Italy was the equal of any political community – and that its history was a living legacy. They anticipated a Third Rome.

Fresh from their victory in the Great War, Fascists sought, through what we now call "masculine protest," to reestablish themselves as heirs of a heroic and vital continuity – from antiquity to the present. They wore the uniforms and bore the arms of an army that had beaten back the enemies from the soil of the fatherland. Their leaders animated them with an anticipation of vast developments, of economic expansion, and cultural revival. There is no question that all that was at the center of Fascism as it mobilized millions.

If we unpack all of that, we also find a collection of judgments that give substance to Fascism's convictions concerning modern liberalism and representative democracy. During the last quarter of the nineteenth century, both French and Italian syndicalists deplored "demo-liberalism" – for a variety of reasons. They argued that modern liberalism had made the heroes of yesteryear, the passive, and self-indulgent, narcissists of today. They argued that demo-liberalism corrupted all those virtues in which humanity had gloried. They were advocates of a self-serving, and mindless skepticism that weakened every fiber that sustained the nation.

Together with that the theoreticians of Fascism made their own pointed judgments concerning the unimaginable malfeasance and lack of fiduciary responsibility that made a mockery of representative democracy. They argued that in liberal-democratic systems, parliaments were markets in which the nation's material wealth, cultural accomplishments, and collective security, were sold and bartered for whatever was offered. Before he became a spokesman for Fascist authoritarianism, Roberto Michels had delivered the case against political liberalism and representative democracy. He was one among many. By the time it was prepared to contest the political power arrangement on the peninsula, Fascism had announced its rejection of "demo-liberalism." While Mussolini, later in his tenure, was prepared to acknowledge the sometimes failures of the authoritarian system he had contrived, he never advocated a return to the standard electoral system fashioned in the liberal tradition. The system cobbled together in the *Repubblica sociale*, during his last years, is evidence enough of that.

Fascism chose an authoritarian and elitist system to govern Italy during its drive to industrial maturity because it offered maximum control of its population – a population only partially educated to the responsibilities attendant on the arduous drive to economic expansion and industrial sophistication. In that sense, Fascism was both a mass-movement that sought reaffirmation of the rights of a proletarian nation, *and* it was profoundly opposed to liberal representative democracy.

It was Gentile who made the latter objection an irreducible component of Fascist social convictions. In that sense, Fascism's opposition to demo-liberalism stood independent of its basic, developmental, economic concerns. Gentile was a convinced collectivist. The democracy of the advanced industrial nations he saw as a threat to the moral future of human kind. He saw in Fascism a system of rigorous, if flexible, control that would guide the human spirit to a fulfillment impossible in any other alternative.

*You argue that having an appropriate project term to charac-
terize Italian Fascism provides perspective on the entire Ventennio. Could you elaborate on that?*

My argument is that in acknowledging Fascism's stated intention to rapidly develop the industry and the general economy of the peninsula, we immediately appreciate its policy
of controlling labor, restricting the growth of wages, as well
as assuming more and more control over the activities of
the entrepreneurial community. Every economy, with very
rare exceptions, during its initial stages of growth, essentially employs the same tactics. Identifying Fascism as a
member of a family of developmental regimes affords perspective and allows us a more comprehensive and objective
understanding of the system.

First of all, recognizing the essential properties of the system allows us to relate it to contemporary political systems
as well as those of the past. Placing Fascism in context supplies us with insights that otherwise would have made its
behavior seem either arbitrarily oppressive or grossly dysfunctional. Ever since the industrial revolution, the international community has witnessed several realities: (1) those
nations that were the first to commence the process, and
achieve some measure of economic development, gained a
presence that allowed their dominance over other communities that remained economically retrograde. The economically advanced communities could deploy larger quantities
of military hardware, employed by populations better educated, that allowed them to dominate others – to purloin
their resources, to change the conditions of trade to favor
themselves, and to render colonial populations subservient.

As a consequence, whenever conditions allowed, the less developed communities were soon inspired to attain the level of economic, and specifically, industrial development that would reduce their vulnerability. Nations like Spain, that failed to develop as rapidly as their immediate competitors, were quickly reduced to the status of secondary actors. Great Britain and France, and subsequently Germany and the United States – all of whom enjoyed some measure of success in their developmental efforts, emerged as "world powers."

Certainly by the nineteenth century, the peoples of the world had become aware of the prevailing dynamics. An entire group of revolutionaries made their appearance. They appeared in bountiful numbers in Europe. Karl Marx and Friedrich Engels were among them. But they were not alone. Giuseppe Mazzini was a notable figure. Whatever might be said of his efforts, it is clear that he anticipated an Italy that would rise up against its tormentors, to unite in infrangible unity behind a government that would serve as both its "heart" and its "mind," in order to work in selfless labor to make the nation the equal of any other. He foresaw a nation in which loyalty was its religion, and in which sacrifice was to be expected. He anticipated a rapid development of its retrograde economy.

Mazzini was only one among the many – they were revolutionaries, under the dominance of "plutocratic" powers, who sought to achieve their respective nation's reactive development. One need only look to the Far East, to Japan and China, to find revolutionaries who also called on their nation to unite in absolute unity, obedience and sacrifice, in order to commence a program that would create a population and an economy capable of defending the essential interests of their community in a highly competitive world.

Mazzini was only one of the many revolutionaries who anticipated that a rapid development of their nation's economy required nationalism as its inspiration, and a kind of religious devotion of its citizens to the cause in order to sustain the enterprise. The features of such a system had been broadcast since the very beginning of the industrial revolution. At the very commencement of the process, the revolution that freed the North American colonies from the dominance of England, articulated a program of economic, and specifically industrial, development. It was Alexander Hamilton who drafted a developmental plan for the United States. In the years that were to follow the political system allowed substantial freedom of enterprise – which implied that labor could not organize in its own defense. In such a system, wages were considered the simple consequence of competition – forcing "free" labor to compete directly with slave labor to fix income levels. Even after the manumission of slaves, organizing labor in the United States was still considered an "obstruction of trade" – and treated as a criminal infraction. It was clear that the system was going through the preliminary phase of "capital accumulation" – collecting the capital for the rapid expansion of the industrial base. Classical Marxism was very explicit in identifying such a period of preliminary capital accumulation at the commencement of the development of a commodity economy. It is to be observed, in various forms, in all communities embarking on economic growth and modernization. As will be indicated, the institutional and political conditions governing that accumulation would vary according to prevailing circumstances.

Thus, primitive capital accumulation looked very different in Japan after the Meiji Restoration than it did in the post-revolutionary North American colonies. Slavery was not institutionalized in the traditional agrarian economy of Japan, although agrarian labor was bound by traditional constraints unknown in North America. Moreover, Japan did not have an institutional party system, so that population control would have to be exercised by more traditional means. The Japanese turned to a *politicized religion*, Shintoism, to instill obedience and a readiness to sacrifice among the general population.

The processes involved in their respective programs of economic growth and development differed among the developing nations in substantial fashion. The industrial development of Japan, for example, was precipitated by the impact of the Western imperialist powers on a nonindustrial, traditional society – a circumstance that molded the Japanese response. What made Fascism different was a consequence of the conditions in which development was to proceed. Given the extraordinary costs of the Great War, and the social unrest it generated in a community suffering a population density that exceeded that of almost every nation in Europe, Fascism had to assume measures of strict control. Labor unrest had to be systematically controlled, the financial system stabilized, and general guidance provided. The academic analysts of economic growth have attempted to identify the peculiar stage of growth when one might expect the appearance of a system sharing the defining traits of paradigmatic Fascism. They have not been notably successful. It seems perfectly evident that a developmental regime, undertaken under one or another set of conditions, would display features uniquely its own.

Fascism certainly was singular in a number of ways. Mussolini provided a working definition of Fascism in several places and at several times. In each case, Fascism appears distinctive – but still a member of class of systems bearing a generic resemblance. In 1933, before the Assembly of the National Council of Corporations, he defined the Fascist State as that agency that "carries out the complete organic and totalitarian regulation of production with a view to the expansion of the wealth, political power, and well-being of the Italian people." That, alone, identifies Fascism as non-democratic in essence, distinguishing it from those developmental systems conducted under democratic-liberal auspices as a consequence of their history. But Mussolini went on to specify that the state would be "totalitarian" – so that it was characterized by "organic" control – the instrument of control being the "unitary party."

The minimum characterization of the Fascist State as a developmental dictatorship provides for the following properties: (1) the national developmental intention of an economic system retaining some of the critical properties of the market (part of Mussolini's chosen "circumspection" in dealing with the economy), but "regulated" by state agents. (2) The controls would be "totalitarian"; that is to say, in principle, that the State could intervene through the instrumentalities of the single party wherever it conceived intervention necessary. That allowed sufficient room for the market to provide a rational guide for resource allocation, prices, and wages – all subject to political review. The writings of Alfredo Rocco provide a measure of insight into the dynamics of such a "controlled" system. (The discussion of the system, years later, by Alberto De' Stefani, remains instructive.)

Until about the early 'thirties the generally accepted standardized economic data present a picture of overall economic growth and increasing industrial sophistication in Italy. There was an evident improvement in life conditions virtually everywhere on the peninsula. These were the years antecedent to the "years of consensus" celebrated in De Felice's history of Fascism. The years of consensus marked the transition from one to another period. By the mid-'thirties, the hitherto prevailing international economic arrangements had lapsed into crisis, and political tensions were rising everywhere. Those circumstances seem to have signaled the beginning of an entirely new phase in Fascism's history. Denis Mack Smith cites Fascist efforts at "militarization" of the nation as a response to these developments. He uses that as evidence of Mussolini's betrayal of his promises of enhanced "productivism" as a community aspiration. How can your interpretation of Fascism help us understand this period?

By the beginning of the 1930s, the Fascist program of rapid industrial development and sophistication had produced some notable results – in the electrification of the rail system, and the extension of electricity into the rural areas. That was augmented by the rapid expansion of the peninsula's road system, and the fabrication of one of the most generous social welfare systems in the Europe of the time. Large investments were committed to the development of aircraft design and production, and the period saw the long flights to Asia and the transatlantic crossings. All were seen as palpable evidence of Fascist successes in its developmental programs. Italo Balbo, whose initiatives fostered Italy's successes in the air, clearly stated that the efforts were designed to lift the pall of economic inferiority and national humiliation from the "New Italy." At the same time, Italy entered into the phase of development that economists tend to identify as "the drive to industrial maturity" – a phase having some general characteristics that carry with them important implications.

Nations at that stage of development find themselves facing a set of issues that demand resolution. Those communities emerging from relative backwardness suddenly find themselves requiring natural resources in quantity and quality never before experienced. This becomes particularly serious when the developing community lacks some of the more essential inputs. In the case of England, as an example, the rapid development of more sophisticated industry made greater and greater demands on foreign inputs (in England's case, one special need was for cotton). That drove British merchant vessels, and ships-of-the-line for their protection, far afield. During the process, the superiority of their naval inventory made the British a dominant, expansionist power. The farther British interests extended, the more security was sought. Supported by the military force that accompanied Britain's search for raw materials, London was empowered to set the conditions of trade – that favored its interests. As a consequence of its domination of trade, assured by advanced ships-of-the-line – England become a formidable international military, economic, and cultural force.

In the course of, and in response to, all of this, the North American colonies sought independence from the prevailing constraints on trade imposed by England. Once liberated from the British Crown, the new North American nation sought to secure trade, land and resource access both across the North American continent and the Atlantic. In North America, the newly liberated colonists proceeded to displace the indigenous population through force of arms. In the circumstances they created for themselves, it seems clear that the North Americans sought and enjoyed security in depth, extending their control from one ocean to another. Flanked by oceans and friendly (or militarily weak) powers, the United States could employ its energies almost exclusively in the expansion of its economy.

Japan, conversely, during its early phase of economic growth, finding itself with limited natural resources, a large population, and minimal security in depth, sought to expand into Korea and China in the predictable effort to secure resources and enhance its security perimeter. Each developing community faces a unique set of circumstances upon entering its drive to industrial maturity – and consequently seeks a relatively unique resolution.

This suggests something of the dynamics of communities pursuing rapid economic and industrial growth in an environment dominated by foreign competitors. Fascist Italy, in its first major growth phase, found itself confronted by singular conditions. It sought independence from foreign economic and political influences in its program of rapid material growth and industrial development. As difficult as that was in the political arrangements of the early 1920s, Italy's programs were further burdened by the nation's lack of some of the most basic natural resources required for expansion. Attempting to acquire such resources through trade, in a world system dominated by the "plutocratic powers" was clearly not an attractive prospect. To maintain its political independence, Fascist Italy ultimately sought the necessary resource inputs overseas – in regions as yet unoccupied by the "great powers." It was in this context that Ethiopia was seen as a potential source of critical raw materials for the peninsula, as well as a space that might support Italy's prospective demographic expansion. Many Fascist economists speculated on the abundance of raw materials that would be made available with the conquest and "uplift" of the "empty and retrograde spaces" of Ethiopia (an argument made familiar by North European imperialists – a variation on the theme of the "white man's burden").

More than that, it was argued that ports on the coast of East Africa would offer Italy the prospect of servicing sealines of communication outside the confines of the British controlled Suez. Air transport from Libya to Ethiopia was deemed feasible – and that would provide the developing Italian economy the advantages of trade outside the constraints of British management. Moreover, Italian military power deployed in East Africa might provide advantage in any hypothetical conflict with the major powers.

The Fascist attack on Ethiopia initiated a series of responses on the part of the "demo-plutocracies." Having entirely forgotten their histories as "imperialists," the major industrial nations deemed Fascist Italy an "irresponsibly aggressive power" to be meted summary punishment through sanctions by the world organization. By that juncture the die had been cast. Henceforward, Fascist Italy was to be considered a pariah state, a political community committed to violence as a first recourse in the search for solutions to international conflicts of interest.

As a consequence of those realities, Mussolini had little choice but to transfer assets from the program of rapid economic and industrial growth to the accelerated development of military power. In retrospect it seems clear that the Fascist government attempted to accomplish continued economic growth and industrial development while at the same time attempting the construction of security forces capable of repelling foreign initiatives and projecting power. All of that was at cost. Financial and material resources consumed in the development of a very expensive inventory of modern weaponry necessarily impacted the rate of the nation's economic growth.

One need only reflect on the behavior of other developing nations in something of the same circumstances. Soviet Russia, as early as the late 1920s had already begun to emphasize the development of its armed forces at the expense of the revolutionary nation's standard of living – as well as its investment in specifically economic and industrial development. One of the consequences was famine in large sectors of the agricultural economy, and straitened conditions throughout the Union. Millions were pressed into economic service at essentially subsistence wages in the effort to bridge the requirements of both military and economic rapid development. We now know that millions perished as a consequence. By 1940, Stalin seized the Baltic states and entertained designs on Finland. Did the Soviet program have an "historic mandate" that absolved it of any criticism? In what fashion was its behavior substantially different from that of Fascist Italy?

What emerges when we consider the early history of Mao's China? From the moment of its founding, the People's Republic of China committed itself to both rapid economic development and the accelerated expansion of its military capabilities. The difficulties involved in the effort are evidenced by the fact that the dual process cost China millions of lives through government enforced conditions that resulted in mass starvation. The imposition of excessive labor demands on the general population resulted in millions of unnatural deaths among those in the working population. In retrospect, how would we judge Mao's plans governing China's drive to industrial maturity? Would they be considered "historically vindicated"? How does the program of Fascist Italy fare by comparison?

Both the Soviet Union and the People's Republic of China enjoyed relatively large populations, secure in a vast continental space. They both had the benefit of an abundant resource base. If it is judged that their conduct, which resulted in the death of millions of their citizens in peace time, has historic warrant – what does that imply in terms of our judgment of the conduct of Fascist Italy?

It would seem that only those developing nations that proceed with their drive to industrial maturity in special circumstances avoid the difficulties here reviewed. A nation like South Korea can proceed with its authoritarian program of accelerated growth while strategically insecure because it has had, and to this day has, the firm collateral political and military support of a major power. Similarly, a small, politically authoritarian community like Taiwan finds itself

capable of administering a successful growth program because of the unqualified support of the United States. Other
authoritarian communities, like Hong Kong and Singapore
can undertake their respective programs of economic growth
and development without concern for their existential survival because of the protection of one or another "super
power."

*You seem to suggest that the political and military develop-
ments of the mid-1930s exercised decisive influence on the subsequent character and policies of Fascist Italy. In what sense
do you mean that to have been the case?*

There are very few serious political historians who deny
the importance of Italy's war in Ethiopia on the international standing of Fascism. Until that time, Fascist Italy
was accorded grudging admiration by a considerable number of political leaders, academics, and lay persons in many
demo-liberal communities. Until the occasion of the war,
Mussolini had attempted to cooperate with the industrial
powers of Western Europe in the construction of a "Four
Power Pact" that might stabilize the increasingly uncertain
political future of Europe. The effort came to naught, and
a rising National Socialist Germany changed all the calcu-
lations governing Europe's prospects.

At that time, Mussolini entertained grave misgivings concerning the rise of German military power in Central Europe. The problem was that, in general, neither the British
nor the French seemed prepared to act decisively in the face
of increasing German provocation. The reconstitution of
the German military forces was allowed to proceed with little reaction from London or Paris. In all of this uncertainty,

the Civil War in Spain cast Fascist Italy in the role of a German ally – when it seems reasonably clear that at that point Mussolini's relationship with Germany was still hesitant. While there was talk of cooperation between the two powers – with Germany giving Italy support in its actions in Africa – what that implied was not at all certain.

To seek to make an ally of Franco Spain served both Italy's short and long term goals. It would give Italy access to a sea coast on the Atlantic, outside the routes governed by the British control of Gibraltar. There was also the expectation that Spain might provide facilities for air force deployments – that would provide significant tactical advantage in the event of conflict between Britain and Fascist Italy

Clearly, Germany's defense of Italian initiatives in Ethiopia, together with the tenuous alliance of National Socialist and Fascist forces in Spain, fostered an increasingly intimate diplomatic relationship between Hitler's Germany and Fascist Italy. The process was to conclude with the Anti-Comintern pact and the subsequent "Pact of Steel" – inextricably binding Italy to the fate of Hitler's Germany.

What seems clear in retrospect is that the association of Fascist Italy with National Socialist Germany was a union that reflected a shared bitterness at their treatment by the advanced industrial powers – Italy because it was economically backward and Germany because it had been denied its place among the world powers as a consequence of its defeat in the Great War. Couched in terms of opposition to the Comintern, the Axis powers sought not to further undermine the relationship between the signatories and the demo-liberal powers – but clearly the Western powers entered into the foreign policy assessments of Rome and Berlin. .

Germany and Italy each assumed the posture of a "revisionist" power, with Fascist Italy emphasizing its demands as a "new," "youthful," and "proletarian" contender. Hitler's demands became increasingly restorationist. He undertook the recreation of the German armed forces, violating the restrictions on numbers and weapon systems in the Treaty of Versailles. He also made clear he had irredentist intent – to bring German nationals back into the Reich who had been scattered into neighboring countries at the end of the Great War. Thus, it seems evident that the burgeoning alliance was predicated on the evident immediate interests of the Axis partners, concealing some fundamental incompatibilities that ultimately would negatively impact the very essence of Fascism.

For years Mussolini had grave misgivings concerning Hitler. For his part, Hitler had unstinted admiration for Mussolini. On several occasions he insisted on the implausibility that without the Blackshirts there never would have been any Brownshirts. To put a fine point on his evident admiration, Hitler had a bust of Mussolini placed in the foyer of Nazi headquarters in Munich – the only political figure to be so honored. On the occasion of his state visit to National Socialist Germany in September 1937, Hitler employed every device to politically seduce Mussolini. Hitler conducted military exercises calculated to demonstrate German military superiority. It was an orchestrated success, and it is evident that Mussolini was overwhelmed. He abandoned all reserves concerning the new Reich. Thereafter, Mussolini chose to consider the National Socialist/Fascist alliance sacrosanct.

Until the mid-1930s, Mussolini remained largely indifferent to Hitler's blandishments. Thereafter, the combination of Italy's increasing preoccupation with its economic and security interests in the Mediterranean and East Africa, and the growing opposition of the British and French to Mussolini's pursuit of those interests, rendered Mussolini more susceptible to the possibilities of a German-Italian alliance of convenience. The Rome-Berlin alliance gave Italy increased confidence in the pursuit of its economic and security goals in the Mediterranean. Its treatment of Albania, as an example, constituted one instance of that increased confidence. Once Fascism came to power, Albania made available to Italian industry, by treaty, some of its vital natural resources. By the end of the 1930s, however, the British foreign office apparently persuaded King Zog to terminate the agreements. With Britain and France distracted by German efforts at resolving its irredentist problems in Czechoslovakia and Poland, Mussolini was emboldened and invaded Albania – not only to ensure continued access to the sought after raw materials, but to exclude further British penetration into Italy's defense perimeter. Albania was essential to the control of the Adriatic. With British forces based in Egypt, Malta, and Gibraltar, Rome sought to deny English forces access to the Balkan defense region. At that point in time, Germany extended Fascist Italy strategic support.

Together with German moves in Austria, Czechoslovakia, and Poland, the new allies were deemed threats to public peace and international order. Europe had entered the preparatory phase for the advent of the Second World War.

While you speak of the German-Italian alliance that preceded the Second World War as the result of "contingent interests" on the part of the signatories, was there not a more profound affinity that made the Axis pact something more than an alliance of convenience?

That was clearly the real or pretended governing conviction of the Allied powers throughout the Second World War. Through the entire conflict, they insisted that their opponents were united on the most fundamental principles. So convinced of the essential affinities of Fascism and National Socialism, the Allies identified the war as a "War Against Fascism" – as though all the opponent powers were "fascists" – united in creed and deed. Even the Japanese were swept into the imagery. There were German "fascists," Japanese "fascists," and Italian fascists – all protagonists in a war against "democracy" (even the Soviet Union was presented as an "incipient democracy"!). The conviction that there was one demon enemy, intrinsically evil, that sought only to murder and enslave – provided the Allied powers with precious propaganda advantage

The fact is that neither the Japanese nor the Germans considered themselves "fascists." National Socialism had an entirely different ideological foundation, and was the spawn of an entirely different national aspiration. In reality, it took but little research and reflection to provide evidence that there was very little common "essence" shared by Fascist and National Socialist doctrine – and there was even less similarity in overall Fascist and National Socialist conduct. Other than select institutional features: the leadership of "charismatics," the dominance of a single-party, and the centrality of the absolute state, there were more doctrinal differences and variations in behavior than commonalities between the two systems.

Fascist doctrine was a coherent amalgam of various streams of thought that had matured in Italy prior to, and during, the Great War. Mussolini came to power animated by an evocative creed predicated on the primacy of the nation, the myth of its fulfillment as a Third Rome, and a productivist commitment shared with Futurists, revolutionary Nationalists, and National Syndicalists, united with the neo-idealism of Gentile, Fascism assumed control of the Italian peninsula prepared with the essentials of both doctrine and program. It commenced with a public policy that understood all the material interests of component individuals and corporations as subject to the ultimate surveillance of the state. The very first tentative pieces of legislation sought to reduce labor's right to strike and the right of entrepreneurs to allocate resources and choose outcomes. Private property, in fact, was seen as a public responsibility, rather than an individual right. These convictions were partially codified in the Carta del lavoro of 1927 and their institutional form was projected by Ugo Spirito in the Corporative Conference in Ferrara in 1932. The effort was made to regularize the "social concept of property" – to emphasize corporative function and responsibility rather than individual prerogatives.

The pursuit of a "Fascist social order" was a serious undertaking. By the time of the "years of consensus," significant strides had been made. Both Mussolini and Gentile contributed aid and insight into Spirito's efforts at institutionalizing the "corporative state." It was the dramatic change in the international environment that complicated the move forward.

The situation surrounding the expression and the application of National Socialist thought was fundamentally different. In the first place, National Socialist doctrine was the product of one man's reflections. National Socialism was the creation of Adolf Hitler; its doctrine was a system of beliefs fashioned by him out of his reading of social Darwinist literature so popular in Europe in the years leading to the Great War. There is every reason to believe Hitler when he insisted that the essentials of his political beliefs were already assembled by the time of the war. He maintained that he began his political career possessed of a doctrine he had already put together, which he had no occasion thereafter to alter.

Virtually the entirety of National Socialist doctrine is contained in Hitler's *Mein Kampf*. More than that, almost every policy pursued by Germany during the Second World War is found there –at least in principle. Certainly, there were German theoreticians who attempted to supplement the account in *Mein Kampf* with references to the German philosophical and historicist literature that was so abundantly available. There was a tentative effort to associate Martin Heidigger with National Socialist thought, but nothing was to come of it. National Socialist thought was, and remained through its existence, the thought of Adolf Hitler. The claim that Alfred Rosenberg served as "the philosopher of National Socialism" was never really plausible. When Rosenberg completed his *Mythus des 20. Jahrhunderts*, Hitler held it an impressive intellectual product, but not an expression of official National Socialist doctrine. For Hitler, there was apparently but one source for National Socialist doctrine – and that was *Mein Kampf.*

Hitler makes mention of Houston Stewart Chamberlain in his *Table Talks* and his correspondence. There are almost casual references to Friedrich Nietzsche and Arthur Schopenhauer – but no one pretends that Hitler's thought was in any serious fashion dependent on that of Chamberlain, Nietzsche, or Schopenhauer. Whatever Hitler took from these thinkers was transformed immediately into the simple social Darwinism of *Mein Kampf.* Hitler was the author of his system of beliefs, and the architect of his New Order.

There are a great many possible sources for Hitler's ideas. I have cited some in my treatments of National Socialist doctrine – but the references remain fugitive. Any serious effort to document the source of Hitler's ideas leaves one with a sense of intellectual dissatisfaction. His beliefs are composed of vast historical generalizations that are left unconfirmed except by an appeal to anecdotes. Allusions are made to cosmic purposes for which no confirmation can be forthcoming. In fact, Hitler never pretended to have written an academic treatise. He insisted that he did not write for the academic skeptic – he wrote for those comrades in faith who were already committed. As a consequence, one finds neither footnotes nor source citations in any of his writings or in his speeches. At the conclusion, we are left with the singular thought of a singular individual: Adolf Hitler.

Upon assuming power, National Socialism almost immediately sought to implement the program given explicit expression in *Mein Kampf.* Its critical center was a handful of convictions concerning biological race. Hitler held that

89

one race, and one race alone, possessed the genetic talent to produce and sustain a complex civilization. Hitler made clear that *science* had convinced him that every major civilization was the product of "Germanic" (or "Aryan") blood, and as the quantity of that blood diminished in the population, there was a *causally* related decline in the survival capacity of the subject civilization. Hitler might have cited the works of German anthropologists to support his case – but he did not.

Out of Hitler's stream of consciousness doctrine two critical obligations are identified as definitive: (1) protection of the Germanic (or Aryan) blood that is the sustaining necessity for the survival of civilization; and (2) defense against the Jews, a people Hitler identified as the agents of societal corruption and decay. Both of these enjoinments constituted the critical moral imperatives of National Socialism. Not only did Hitler initiate programs to satisfy those imperatives upon his accession to power, but they became articles of faith for the armed defenders of the system. The SS (Schutzstaffel) became the standard bearer for the system – and its doctrines were race-based. Whatever else National Socialism may have been, its animating doctrines were indisputably and unqualifiedly racist.

None of that was to be found in Fascist doctrine. In his youth, Mussolini had read much of the available racist literature generated among North European intellectuals – only to deny its credibility. Until the mid-1930s, Mussolini was dismissive of any attempt to conceive race, in whatever guise, as an historic determinant. That there were those who imagined race to be of historic significance he attributed to a sentiment generated by circumstances. He spoke of a preoccupation with race as having a psychological origin, as little more than an overt expression of a felt sentiment. In his discussions with Emil Ludwig, Mussolini made several things clear: (1) he was familiar with the major pieces of theoretical literature that provided the substance of National Socialist race theory; and (2) he was prepared to dismiss the work in its entirety. He certainly did not lend it any credence. In effect, until the mid-1930s, there was little in Fascist doctrine that might be identified as racist. A great deal would have to intervene before Fascism would broadcast its own "racist convictions" – when Party theoreticians would publish a "Manifesto of Fascist Racism." Even with its appearance in July, 1938, however, little was resolved. Italians were somehow deemed "Aryans" with a "Nordic orientation" – assertions more notable for their vagueness, and lack of conviction, than for their illumination.

National Socialist thinkers, following the practice found in *Mein Kampf* used the terms "Aryan," "Germanic," and "Nordic" (usually indiscriminately) as racial designations. Very few provided an observable criterial list for any of the terms employed – that would allow the identification of given individuals with a particular racial category. (The clear exception was Hans F. K. Günther whose insistence on precision resulted in his identification of over ninety five percent of the population of Germany as being composed of persons who displayed evidence of racial intermixture. Virtually all Germans were racial "hybrids" – there was little "purity" to be found among them.)

Fascist "racial doctrine" contributed nothing to the ill-contrived "biological" racism of National Socialism. Those theoreticians who put together the racial doctrine of Fas-

Stalin's Bolshevism. Fascist theoreticians took a measure of pride in the fact that Soviet Russia had taken on more and more specifically Fascist traits with the passage of time and with increasing responsibilities.

The alliance with National Socialist Germany transformed Fascist Italy from a revolutionary state to one that was "criminal." The Allied powers immediately deemed the system one that glorified violence and war – essentially pursuing war for its own sake. All the subtleties of Sorel and Panunzio concerning the use of force and violence in revolution and war disappeared in the heavy handed treatment of Allied critics. Quotations from turn-of-the-century social Darwinists on the "purifying" and "eugenic" properties of war were repeated and the sentiment attributed to "fascists." By the end of the Second World War, Fascism had been transformed into a system of beliefs that sought only destruction and bloodshed.

Granting much of that, it does seem that there were "radicals" among the membership and the elite of the Partito nazionale fascista (PNF) who published outrageous opinions that seemed to justify war and racial oppression. Among Fascists, moreover, there were advocates of "right-wing" and "left-wing" variations of the official doctrine – all of which left a confusing impression of what Fascists were understood to believe.

All of that is substantially true. The semi-official *Difesa della razza*, for example, regularly contained incendiary articles (by relatively unknown theoreticians) concerning war and human conflict. It also contained scurrilous articles about the Jews as a "race." They were charged with every conceivable infamy – which, if true, made them the proper objects of public abuse.

The *Difesa della razza*, together with the abundance of similar literature, was a direct result of the attempt, undertaken immediately before the coming of the war, to reduce the ideological distance between Fascism and National Socialism. In the course of those efforts, Mussolini permitted intellectuals to publish opinions that confused and undermined established Fascist opinion on a variety of sensitive topics. He permitted, for example, a curious book on "spiritual racism", written by Julius Evola, to appear in Germany with the misleading suggestion that it represented Fascist doctrinal opinions.

None of those efforts had the sought effect. German race theory would not be modified by any products emanating from Italy. There is no evidence that the intellectual leadership of National Socialism was in any way influenced by the Fascist efforts. Evola, for example, was dismissed by National Socialist authorities as a "reactionary" whose views on any subject were not to be taken seriously (years before, major Fascist intellectuals had made the same judgment).

All of this was harbinger of much more tragic things to come. The evidence indicates that Hitler was not particularly interested in having Fascist Italy as a partner on the battle field. He anticipated Fascist Italy, as an involved neutral, tying down British and French forces in the Mediterranean and North Africa, freeing German forces to rampage over Western Europe.

Mussolini was of a different mind. He was certain of German military ascendancy, and that the war that Hitler wanted would be of short duration. He was also convinced that without the direct participation of Italian forces in the anticipated victory, Rome would not have a seat at the deliberations following the war's conclusion. He was prepared to commit Italian armed forces to battle. The first problem was that Mussolini had no idea of the scope of Hitler's plans. National Socialist Germany never shared its strategic plans with its Italian ally. The second major problem that beset Italy's entry into the war as a belligerent, turned on the reality that at the time Hitler chose to embark on the conflict, Italian industry had not matured sufficiently to adequately equip forces in the field. Almost everywhere, Fascist forces were under-powered and under-gunned. Fascist aircraft, though maneuverable, were not equipped with engines that could provide the power that would sustain them in modern air combat. Italian armor, in general, was too light for modern armored warfare. Italian forces had too few artillery pieces disposable for combat. The entire logistics structure of the armed forces left a great deal to be desired. The navy was Italy's most capable military arm, and it never seemed fully disposed to engage its opponents in combat. In substance, Fascist Italy was not ready for involvement in a modern conflict.

Given their material limitations, Italians comported themselves well in combat. Both enemies and allies attested to that. But from the opening of conflict, Fascist forces suffered a series of disabling defeats. In North Africa, German ground forces and air support were necessary to contain the enemy. In Greece and the Balkans, once again German forces were required to avoid a Fascist defeat.

All of this undermined support for the Regime. By the time Hitler decided to invade the Soviet Union, popular support in Italy for the war against the Allies had dwindled. The devastating attack on the fleet in Taranto, the loss of the hard won colonies in East Africa, the American entry into the conflict, the inability to resist the Anglo-American forces in North Africa, and the paralyzing casualties on the Eastern Front, all critically impaired Italian resistance.

The final phase of doctrinal development in Fascist Italy – suffering as it did the catastrophic defeats inflicted by the overwhelming power of the Allied forces – was almost pathological. There were those prepared to abandon the historic doctrine and assume more of the belief system that inspired National Socialists (a significant number of young Italians volunteered for enlistment in the SS). By the time of the *Repubblica sociale di Salò*, Fascists collected around themselves a wide variety of advocates ranging from those with the traditional convictions that informed the *Ventennio*, to insistent enthusiasts of corporativism that appeared in the form of a modified socialism (Corridoni's final national syndicalist essays were republished), together with a National Socialist element enflamed by a lunatic anti-Semitism. On the margins, one of the founders of the Italian Communist Party was to be found. Mussolini, supported by a pervasive German presence, held the entire variegated company together. Within the vast and despairing confusion, there were those, like Gentile, who sought to hold Fascism to its historic responsibilities.

The Second World War was not only a military debacle for Fascist Italy – it corroded its ideological substance. Those who survived the vindictive mass killings at the end of the war found themselves aliens in their own land. If they sought shelter among their own, they found themselves among "fascists" advocating, among other anachronisms, political terror and indiscriminate violence, with the intent to overthrow the political arrangements that the Allied victory had imposed upon them. Others found themselves members of small intellectual circles reviewing, once again, the argument for a corporative reform of Italy's economic system. Some of these survivors picked up the threads of "right radicalism" that had surfaced during Fascism's long defeat. Others were the "left-wing" advocates of that "socialistoid" belief system that attempted to appeal to Italy's working class in Fascism's final hours. All of these views animated a multiplicity of small groups, each bearing a fragment of a belief system by that time displaying no semblance of coherence. In effect, the lost war had shorn Fascism of its doctrinal integrity. The "neofascism" that followed was not only lacking in intellectual substance; it was bereft of potential. In the postwar political environment there was no space for such a "fascism." The most effective of the postwar "neofascist" organizations never netted more than a small percentage of support among Italians. It languished on the political periphery until, by the end of the century, the world, and Italy in it, had changed dramatically.

What finally emerged when "neofascism" acknowledged the prevailing reality was not a fascism at all. It was an essentially conservative political movement, committed to representative government that rejected elements of the "welfare state." The transmogrified "fascists" of the new century were the advocates of individual responsibility, financial accountability, and economic growth. Its members did not reject historic Fascism, but they acknowledged its historic demise. They acknowledged the post-Fascist character of Italy and the Italians. It would appear, as Ernst Nolte suggested, that we have witnessed the close of the "Fascist epoch."

You seem to argue that Italian Fascism is an historic relic, a product of the past, having no interest or relevance either for the present or the future. It would seem that all those features of Fascism, the developmental nationalism, the charismatic leadership, the unitary party, the role of political myth, the ethic of sacrifice and labor, are all exhibits in the museum of antiquities.

Clearly, that cannot all be true. Commentators on current affairs discover "fascism" almost everywhere. If nothing more, "fascism" has become a perennial threat that troubles the sleep of many learned academics. "Fascism" has been discovered in the maunderings of "skin heads," in the lyrics of Hard Rock and "Proletarian" bands. It is found in the violence against immigrants, homosexuals, Jews, and Gypsies. It reveals itself in the vandalism of Jewish cemeteries and the burning of Black churches.

Stated in such a fashion, we all recognize that these evidences of "fascism" are the products of long-standing confusion and incorrigible prejudice. The propaganda produced in such abundance during the passions of the Second World War exercised its influence on the postwar generations of scholars and lay persons. Italian Fascism had become a caricature of itself. It had become a grotesquerie of hateful features. Devoid of intellectual content, it was charged with unspeakable crimes. As a consequence, the search for neofascism anywhere in the world produced only instances of small group behaviors that were essentially criminal at best, and lunatic in substance. Should that be all that is left of historic Fascism, then clearly Fascism is of interest only to those who study the psychologically disturbed and criminally disposed.

What that tells us is that the conception of "fascism" employed after the termination of the Second World War was totally unserviceable. The characterization of Fascism was not in the least credible – and it has been dismissed by most serious academics. The Fascism of Mussolini, Corradini, Olivetti, Gentile, Panunzio, and Spirito had nothing whatever to do with the rag-bag collection of hateful notions that Allied propaganda identified as "fascist." If we choose to look past the prejudicial images, and the simple nonsense that attached itself to the notion in the course of the Second World War, we are immediately impressed by the many political arrangements, found in a variety of places in the postwar world, that irresistibly recall the Fascist governance of prewar Italy.

In undertaking such an assessment, it is necessary to keep several things in mind. (1) Fascism was a belief system composed of many elements, any one of which might appear almost anywhere in the modern world. How many such fascist features a political system would have to display before it is accounted "fascist" is very difficult to establish with much conviction. (2) Even should we accept the suggestion that there was a "fascist epoch" and the we have left it behind, we still have the intellectual obligation – that accompanies all such claims – to determine the date of the commencement, and the date of closing, of the proposed epoch. Stated in such fashion, it immediately becomes clear that neither historians nor social scientists, as a community, are prepared to identify the beginning and the terminus of the "fascist epoch." Some have traced its origins as far back as Plato's *Republic*, others to the reactionaries of the French revolution, and still others to the unravelling of classical Marxism at the beginning of the twentieth century, impacted by the transformative writings of the Italian school of sociology.

If there is a lack of consensus concerning the opening of the "fascist epoch," there clearly is no uniformity of opinion concerning its close. Similar difficulties attend any discussion of historic epochs. The same problems arise with any attempt to isolate the onset or signal the close of the epoch of artistic expressionism, the Renaissance, the industrial revolution, or the "golden age" of ancient Greece. On the basis of individual analysis, each researcher argues for a given date or period for the beginning and close of the era, or epoch, in question. Long familiarity with the history of a time and region allows scholars to isolate the appearance and disappearance of a syndrome of properties that defines a complex historical phenomenon. A similar process is employed in any discussion of "the Fascist epoch." To try to provide a plausible point of origin for such an epoch, one begins with a list of observable traits that would allow the identification of its first appearance. The possession of such a list of criterial traits would further permit the identification of its subsequent close. Whatever one thinks of such a process – whatever else it may be – it clearly is not easy.

Using Italian Fascism as a paradigm case, we search history for instances similar in terms of political properties. While elements of a generic fascism are to be found in a wide variety of places, through early modern history, only in Italy after the Great War did Fascism assume full historic form.

That form is a composite of various traits. If we employ only one, or a select number of traits, to identify "fascism," we may find ourselves overwhelmed with candidates. If we grant, for example, that Fascism, at least in part, was a response to the humiliation suffered by a retrograde economy at the hands of more powerful foreigners, we have isolated a defining trait. We might employ such an insight to identify potential members of the class of "fascisms." Clearly, that would provide us with an embarrassment of candidates. If we only search for political communities suffering the imposture of foreign powers because of a difference in economic development, the North American British colonies immediately come to mind.

Towards the end of the eighteenth century, the British colonies in North America became restless under the weight of British economic and political proscriptions and prescriptions. The colonies felt politically abused and humiliated by their treatment at the hands of their putative "betters." Trading practices and manufacturing initiatives were managed from London. Taxation was a device not only to extract revenue, but imposed to control economic activity. The North American colonists reacted not only to the humiliation suffered at the hands of the economically advanced British, but to the economic exploitation correlative to that abuse.

Should one continue with such an analysis, one would find that it was possible to identify another "fascist" trait in the syndrome of properties that made up the system of beliefs that inspired the North American revolution. If one reviews the discussion typical of the leaders of the revolution concerning the economic development that they expected to follow the revolutionary victory, we recognize one of its major proposals to have been the rapid development of both the agrarian and industrial economy. One need only read Alexander Hamilton's message to the new congress to obtain a sense of that. The fact that Friedrich List – the German critic of Marx and the inspiration for Alfredo Rocco – saw in the new republic, an aspirant to rapid and sophisticated industrialization, suggests that the early American republic met yet another condition for "fascist" enterprise. And yet, there are few (other than Ezra Pound, who sought to compare Mussolini and Thomas Jefferson) who would venture to suggest that the fascist epoch began with the North American revolution of 1776. In fact, that revolution has been more credibly associated with the dawning of the "democratic era."

The American revolution of 1776, on reflection, might be said to display some "fascist" properties, but clearly those properties were incidental to its reality. Those putatively "fascist" characteristics, while significant in some sense, did not determine the major properties of the evolving system.

The fact that the new republic found itself in an environment abundant with raw materials and open space, and free of existential threat, allowed it to choose and function with a representative form of government – allowing the population to be inspired by a civic religion that sought to instill among them the appropriate compliance and labor-intensive disposition. Economic development and industrialization could proceed without the state centered authoritarianism, charismatic leadership, and single-party dominance that typified Fascism.

The fact is that the twentieth century was not to witness another revolutionary, economically retrograde community that enjoyed the advantages of the revolutionaries in North America a century before. By that time, in most circumstances, economic growth and industrial sophistication were compelled to take place in circumstances of scarcity and threat. The result was the appearance of the first Fascism.

If one considers the period in which Fascism arose, one finds its doctrine, its policy, and its practice designed to respond to the demand for complex, yet rapid, economic development. Its representatives, many of them revolutionary Marxists, rejected Lenin's Bolshevism not only because it opposed entry into the Great War, but because it failed to understand its historic obligation: to develop a retrograde economy in a world dominated by those industrially advanced. Lenin, captive of an anachronistic ideology, imagined that revolution could only be a function of both universality and advanced industrial maturity. The classical Marxism that was the original impetus for Leninism was totally inappropriate as a rationale for the rapid development of a retrograde, national economy. As a consequence, it was rejected by Fascist intellectuals who acknowledged a national developmental imperative that arose out of economic and industrial retardation. Lenin's belated effort at a New Economic Policy, an abandonment of classical Marxism, was an unhappy attempt to resolve his dilemma. Whatever the effort, and whatever form it assumed, neither Leninism nor Stalinism provided their system of late development with a means for establishing a method for determining rational pricing, wage, or allocation policies in a national setting. Aware of all that from the very commencement of

104

the Bolshevik experiment, Fascists simply pursued the nationalist and developmental policies advocated by Corridoni, Rocco, Corradini, and Olivetti, allowing the survival of private property and elements of the market to influence wages, prices, allocation, and production – but always under direct or indirect Party control.

Fascists were aware that Bolshevism, essentially abandoning the Marxism of Marx and Engels, had been compelled to assume some of the major political properties of paradigmatic Fascism. Stalin, abandoning all pretense, took on the mantle of a charismatic leader of a single-party, national state, informed by a exclusivist political religion. He made his program one of rapid industrial development. None of this escaped the attention of Fascist intellectuals. Throughout the Ventennio, they pointed out the shared properties of the two systems – but indicated the impairments suffered by Stalinism's attempt to control prices and allocate resources by government fiat. Fascism distinguished itself from Bolshevism and Stalinism not only in its initial and consistent nationalism, but through its allowance of the continued existence of private property, and the survival of critical elements of a competitive market.

If we bear some of this in mind, the years that followed the Second World War take on notable features. Unencumbered by prejudice and prejudgment, the wave of revolutionary political systems that took shape with the "decolonization" that followed the war, took on familiar configuration.

Following the end of the war, vast stretches of Africa and the Middle East assumed revolutionary guise as African and Arab "socialism." Communities, the boundaries of which had been drawn by the "imperialist" powers, suddenly chose to identify themselves as nations driven by the imperative need to economically develop and industrialize. During the postwar period of decolonization, virtually every one of the emergent revolutionary communities opted for unitary, single party governance – each provisioned with a charismatic leader, a minoritarian vanguard elite, a collection of suitable political myths calculated to mass-mobilize masses – all informed by an exclusivist ideology.

Kwame Nkrumah, the charismatic "Savior" (*Osagyefo*) of Ghana, typified the authoritarian leadership of the nationalist and developmental revolutions in Africa. He was inspired by Marcus Garvey – the similarly charismatic leader of Blacks in North America – who claimed to have been a "fascist" before Mussolini. Like Garvey, Nkrumah advocated economic development as a necessity, if Africa was to defend itself from those nations that already enjoyed the power bestowed by advanced industrialization.

Among the political myths intended to inspire the masses of Ghana, was a nationalism, qualified by the recognition that the boundaries of any particular African nation were essentially artificial, drawn at the convenience of colonial masters. A "Pan-African" nation remained a myth for another day. Together with that was the claim that African culture understood the fulfillment of persons to be the consequence of their identification with their community – an identification that the regime would systematically inculcate through a uniform system of public education. Uniformity of belief and behavior was prized above all else

Similar political properties were to be found among almost all the "African socialist" revolutionary states, ranging from Senegal to Tanzania. All were nationalist and developmental, with major sectors of the economy controlled by the unitary party state. Political opposition was muted. All permitted the survival of private property, allowing meaningful sectors of the market to function in the apparent effort to have rational prices available for distributive and allocative purposes. Everywhere, labor was uniformly controlled, and private enterprise strictly administered. All were animated by a deep sense of collective humiliation – the product of offending contact with the advanced industrial nations.

Among the "Arab socialists," the situation was remarkably similar. Gamal Abdel Nasser and Muammar Gaddafi modeled the political features of the charismatic leaders of its "socialism" – and they were those made prominent by "African socialists." Like the African socialists, Arab socialists were animated by a prevailing sense of humiliation rooted in economic backwardness, and cultural inferiority.

The "socialism" of all these revolutionary systems was the same kind of socialism that provided the substance to the revolutionary, and national, syndicalism that was at the center of Mussolini's Fascism. It was the socialism one finds in the ideological legacy of Filippo Corridoni.

One finds some Marxist phrases among the intellectual products of Arab and African revolutionaries, but almost all suppressed the Communist parties within their borders. Whatever the ideologies that ultimately came to identify the systems, none harkened back to the Marxism of Marx or Engels – nor Lenin or Stalin, for that matter. One found among such "socialist" states an opportunism that had them enter into security or economic relations with the Soviet Union, or the nations of the Eastern European bloc, in order, thereby, to reap immediate material advantage. But there was no more doctrinal Marxism, per se, among the ideologues of Arab or African socialism than one might find among the Fascist thinkers of the *Ventennio*, or in the socialistoid policies of the Fascist Republic of Salò.

Once again, because the nationalists of Arab socialism were compelled to deal with a nation largely constructed to conform to the interests of foreign colonizers, their nationalism always threatened to dilate into the distraction of a "pan-Arabism." For years, the "Arab nation" expanded and contracted as political circumstances required. Nonetheless, whatever peculiarities rendered them distinctive, Arab socialist regimes, like those of African socialism, shared a remarkable family resemblance with the Fascism of Mussolini.

None of the Arab or African socialist states were particularly successful. Some were simply overthrown by their own populations or by a conspiracy of foreigners. Some decayed into caricatures of themselves, and others simply devolved into alternative political systems. Whatever their histories, one finds traces of their developmental intentions everywhere – in vast hydroelectric systems, massive dams and water catchments, steel industries, schools, and health service facilities (some reduced to ruins). Whatever the case, that they were "fascistoid" cannot really be denied. They were the result of the demands of the political environment in Africa and the Middle East that followed the conclusion of the Second World War. We did not see the burgeoning of representative political systems – as one might expect with the victory over fascism. We experienced the emergence of political systems displaying all the principal features of Mussolini's Fascism. They were not the product of political persuasion that arose from familiarity with Fascist literature. They were a response to imperatives that arose from the prevailing political circumstances. It was not political literature (except in minor instances) that made Arab or African socialists fascistic. It was the reality of the post-war world. Just as the first Fascism was a response to the conditions that arose on the Italian peninsula at the close of the Great War, so the realities of the world after the Second World War compelled the appearance of those systems that shared its species traits.

That the intellectuals of Arab and African socialism did not publicly identify with Fascism requires no explanation. Most had no familiarity with Fascist literature (except in rare instances), and even if they did, they would be inexcusably foolish to associate themselves with a system that had suffered catastrophic defeat and was universally despised. Nonetheless, anyone not blinded by the prejudices of a war just concluded, could hardly fail to see the shared species properties of Arab and African socialism, and the paradigmatic Fascism which they mirrored.

As postwar Arab socialism disintegrated as a consequence of internal failures and foreign intervention, the flawed systems sought recourse to the alternative we are now witnessing. The desperate effort to lift themselves from the increasing humiliation of further defeat from the industrialized powers has produced the suicidal ideology of "jihadism" – predicated on simple, self-destructive violence. It is a murderous ideology without constructive purpose. It does not aspire to economic or social development. Its revolutionary model is the Islamic society of the eighth century. It is an anachronism, having no chance of political success, promising only death and/or repression.

If a "Fascist continuity" is to be sought, it will not be found in the desperate "jihadism" of failed Arab states. If such a continuity is to be found, it would have to surface among revolutionary systems that have chosen "fascist" modalities to achieve the ends of rapid industrialization and militarization. We would expect to find, once again, the charismatic leader, leading the unity party, in an administered economy, all in a nation that aspires to a redress of perceived grievances.

You speak of a "Fascist continuity" that is rarely spoken of. I am not aware that there has ever been a discussion of such continuity among scholars. I have never even heard of such a discussion among the past or current advocates of "neofascism." First of all, could you explain why that is the case? Furthermore, why would such continuity be of any interest to the contemporary world?

If you accept my thesis that the study of Italian Fascism has been hopelessly compromised by the distortions produced by the passions and propaganda necessities of one of the most destructive wars in human history, you can understand the inability of most contemporaries to perceive the kind of continuities of which I speak. Most academics and lay persons have been made accustomed to accepting instances of vandalism in synagogues and attacks on immigrant hostels as evidence of "Fascist continuities." Only such continuities are recognized. Product of the notions applied to Fascism during the exigencies of war, they preclude alternatives. Most of the historic substance of Fascism has been lost in the process. Conflated with National Socialism – all of its complex and distinctive doctrinal beliefs and active policies no longer engage academic attention. Fascism has been left bereft of definition.

Neither those of the immediate post-war generation nor those of subsequent generations had any motive to try to restore the actual content of defeated Fascism. Any such effort could easily be construed an "apology of Fascism" – an activity that constituted an actionable criminal offense in post-war Italy. Among Anglophone scholars there was no more reason to attempt a reassessment of Fascism. The United States and Britain had suffered at the hands of Fascism – and their scholars had little incentive to attempt a balanced and more objective review of what had become the "standard" dismissal.

Not until the appearance of "historical revisionists" – such as Renzo De Felice, Stanley Payne, Ernst Nolte, and Zeev Sternhell – did "Fascist studies," as an academic discipline, begin a studied reassessment of the doctrinal and political history of Italian Fascism. While resistance from those who had become wedded to the conviction that Fascism had been little more than a moral outrage, more and more scholars sought to suspend judgment until the entire two decades of Fascism had been carefully considered.

The complacency of established scholarship, the natural conservatism of fixed opinion, and the rancor of a tragic war, all conspired against any general reconsideration of the entire Fascist sequence. While revisionists produced works of impressive scholarship, members of the traditional Left, well established in American, British, French, and German universities, continued to reiterate the judgments born of the war. While some revisionists explored the implications of their revisions of Fascist history, most occupied themselves with the difficult task of furthering the reevaluation of their time-specific subject matter.

While there were those prepared to suggest that some of the post-war Arab and African dictatorships seemed to display more fascist than socialist traits, their suggestions did not fuel much discussion. It was not considered politically correct, for example, to associate Black revolutionaries with something as objectionable as Fascism. "Socialist," or "Marxist" connections were acceptable although neither the African nor Arab revolutionary systems had anything in them that spoke to the doctrinal or political substance of either.

All of that has become clearer in retrospect. At the time, historical studies were clouded by prevailing convictions. Illustrative instances are not difficult to find. In reviewing China studies, for example, studies that covered more than half the twentieth century, we have a case in which intellectual and institutional constraints, born of long standing bias, worked their effects on scholarship.

Even before the coming of the European war in 1939, Anglophone scholars had written extensively about the revolution in China. Since 1911, China had been roiled by revolutionary activity. Originally spontaneous, the followers of Sun Yat-sen, the leader of the nation's dissidents, sought to collect around themselves all the forces committed to the overthrow of the Qing Dynasty and the making of a "New China."

Very little could be anticipated concerning the revolutionary prospects of Sun and his followers. Equally little was known of the participant groups, or their leaders, who undertook the seizure of power. Even less was known of their political intentions. Nonetheless, American scholars quickly began to render judgment. In general, most were positive. Most Americans, in principle, objected to the Chinese ruling class. It was considered primitive and retrograde. It was known to suppress and brutalize those who sought to reform the system. Sun, himself, early in his career, was threatened with the death penalty by the dynasty. In general, most American and British scholars tended to welcome the forced departure of China's dynastic rulers.

Sun made himself still more attractive to Americans by insisting that he intended to introduce a system of popular representation in China – much like that practiced in the United States. He intended, as well, to modernize his backward homeland, bringing it into the twentieth century. To accomplish all that, he appealed to the advanced industrial nations, particularly Britain and the United States. At the time, neither was disposed to render any substantive aid.

In revolutionary China, while the dynasty had been displaced, the revolution itself lacked definition. Although Sun briefly assumed the role of president of what was a new republic, some of the traditional military set him aside and attempted to restore dynastic rule. Sun's response was to organize his current and potential followers into what took on the properties of a modern political party. His new party, the Chinese Nationalist Party (*Kuomintang*), pursuing a fully articulated doctrine, came to dominate much of southern China. From there, Sun's intention was to expand his political control over the totality of the nation.

Sun's doctrine, components of which had been formulated as early as the turn of the century, focused on three prin-

Stalin assumed the leadership of the Bolsheviks and Chiang Kai-shek became *Tsungtsai,* the charismatic leader of Sun's Nationalists.

Chiang quickly became suspicious of the nascent Chinese Communist Party and moved to eliminate it and its members as contenders for power in China. In the course of his efforts, a substantial part of the membership of the small Communist Party was destroyed. What that accomplished – other than the elimination of the immediate threat posed by the presence of the Chinese Communist Party – was to convince Anglophone scholars that Chiang, and his Nationalists were of the political "Right," and looked suspiciously like the Fascism that had recently made its appearance on the Italian peninsula.

Thereafter, irrespective of all the permutations that followed the complex course of Chinese politics through the years beginning with the first efforts of the Nationalists to economically develop the nation, through the Japanese invasion, and then the Second World War – irrespective of the official position of the government of the United States – most American scholars regularly spoke of Chiang and his Nationalists as "fascists." As a result, when Mao Zedong, the charismatic who led the Chinese Communist Party, defeated the Nationalists and declared China a communist republic in 1949, there was satisfaction among many American academicians and China scholars. Once again, "fascism" had been defeated by a "progressive" revolutionary opponent.

For China, the years that followed were tragic. Mao had learned a great deal from Sun, and for years insisted that his program was that of the *Sanminchui.* What quickly came to distinguish Mao's program from that of Sun was not

116

only the rejection of representative democracy as an acceptable political form, but the manner of achieving economic and industrial development. Mao chose to mercilessly drive the Chinese into "Great Leaps" in constructive achievement. Dams and irrigation systems were to be built by politically mobilized human effort, unassisted by machinery. Steel mills were to be similarly constructed by unskilled human effort. Thousands of "backyard furnaces" were put together in the effort to produce quantities of steel that would exceed the productivity of Great Britain. The production of foodstuffs, in turn, was to be employed in the foreign purchase of necessary resource supplements. In the course of this frenzied activity perhaps as many as thirty million Chinese died unnatural deaths from political violence, starvation, illness, and overwork. In the political reaction that followed, more than a million perished. The "Cultural Revolution" not only consumed lives, but destroyed a great deal of the nation's cultural heritage. In the course of the political violence, "Red Guards" were pitted against "Red Guards" until finally, the military was forced to quell the fighting and assume control.

Out of that disorder, a political competitor emerged: Deng Xiaoping. He was appalled by the death and destruction Mao's "Great Leap" had left in its wake. He was familiar with the economic recommendations of Sun Yat-sen – and was the advocate of an alternative to Mao's economic policies. Even before the death of the "Chairman," Deng led an opposition that sought to ensure that no further "great leaps" would befall the suffering people of China.

Upon Mao's death in 1976, after some political infighting, Deng assumed the responsibilities of ruling a China that had only recently emerged from political instability – and which trembled on the brink of economic collapse. The subsequent story is reasonably well known. Deng restored stability together with substantial property rights to the citizens of China. He allowed the individual accumulation of wealth and the generation of personal profit. The reappearance of profit brought with it the restoration of significant sectors of the market. Market mechanisms allowed the rational allocation of resources, and profits signaled where investments in production were to be made. For more than two decades China enjoyed a double digit rate of economic growth. Millions of peasants were urbanized and millions more left the ranks of the impoverished and enjoyed, for the first time in China's history, an approximation of a moderately comfortable standard of life.

At this point, a question urges itself upon us. How is the Chinese "second revolution" of Deng to be characterized? It is a system that institutionalized the dominant single-party state. The mass-based party is led by a self-selected elite which, in turn, is dominated by a charismatic. Although the charisma is a form of institutionalized charisma, its function is that of all such leadership. The charismatic leader shapes and administers the official ideology of the system. Very early into the post-Maoist changes, Deng was celebrated as the principal theoretician of the Chinese Communist Party. From the retrospective of several decades, it has become clear that the pragmatic, goal directed rationale that directed the political and economic activities of the Chinese Communist Party under Deng was certainly not Marxist either in spirit or content. Whatever its "socialism," it has described its system as a "socialism" at its formative stages.

It is a "socialism" that renders labor subject to the control of a dominant, single, political party. It is a "socialism" that allows wide differences in the levels of income. It is a "socialism" that welcomes foreign capitalists to invest in, and profit from, native Chinese industries. It is a "socialism" that provides tariff advantages to foreigners in order to stimulate the export of goods to overseas markets. It is a "socialism" that affords foreign entrepreneurs special privileges in Chinese law.

In foreign policy, contemporary China is stridently irredentist. It insists on the restoration of "lost lands" – lost to "unequal treaties" and "imperialist aggression." It has mounted an increasingly impressive military. It has constructed elements of a survivable nuclear capability, a modern army, air force, and navy. It has confronted the Japanese in the East China Sea, and a clutch of nations in the South China Sea – all over territorial claims. It threatens the democratic republic of Taiwan, the last redoubt of the Chinese Nationalist Party. It has broadcast claims that originate in the times of the Ming dynasty – that potentially extend China's territorial claims far to its west.

None of this is reminiscent of Marxism in any of its variants. It is clearly "fascistoid." Any reasonably informed and objective observer would conclude as much. And there have been many. Among academics in the United States disappointed leftists have lamented the passing and transcendence of Maoism. More recently, uncommitted scholars have recognized the non-Marxist and Fascist features that distinguish today's China. Not much has been made of the recognition, largely because many American businesses profit from the "China trade" and seek to avoid "controversy." American politicians, apparently influenced by business interests, have turned a blind eye to the "human rights" violations of the authoritarian system. There has been an allowance of aggressive Chinese activity all along its periphery. What seems evident in all of this is the realization that the politics and policies of China are not the product of Marxist doctrine, but a result of the configuration of problems with which it has had to deal.

At this point, there are considerations that urge themselves upon us. We have reviewed something of the history of Italian Fascism. We have argued that Italian revolutionaries, initially convinced Marxists, transformed their doctrine to address the immediate problems that faced their economically backward nation on the eve of the Great War. The result was Fascism. The genius of the Italian revolution was its ready acknowledgment of what was necessary to achieve parity with their "plutocratic" opponents. They were prepared to abandon or transform the ideology they had previously embraced. What emerged was the first Fascism. Its features, by this time, are too familiar to require rehearsal. What we observe in China is a very similar process – that has extended itself over time.

The China of the contemporary world is governed by an ideology that has as its central myths the primacy of nationalism, the history of China as the Central Kingdom, the "hundred years of humiliation" that energized the revolution, the "Long March" that inspired continued struggle, and the conviction that the party possesses the incontrovertible truths that will lead to the rebirth of an exceptional people.

We have seen and experienced all this before. The nature and precondition of revolution had been intuited, not by orthodox Marxists of whatever sort, but by the national syndicalists, and developmental nationalists of the pre-war years in Italy. In 1933, when Mussolini addressed visiting Asian students in Rome, he spoke to them of shared revolutionary incentives. He told them he understood their revolutionary elan. He saw it as the natural product of having been relegated to the inferior role of a market for foreign industrialized goods, and reduced to the source of raw materials for foreign manufactories. He said he understood their irrepressible desire to restore their nation to the status of an equal in the community of nations. He told them that it was all that which originally inspired and continued to inspire Fascists.

Fascist intellectuals regularly acknowledged the Fascist traits that surfaced in China during the long years of its revolution. They saw its features in the policies and practices of Chiang's Nationalists. After the disappearance of historic Fascism, some of its most prominent intellectuals saw familiar features in the China of Mao Zedong. Ugo Spirito wrote copiously of those features after his visit to the People's Republic. Bruno Zoratto recognized Fascist features in the governance of Taiwan as well mainland China.

Today, there can be little doubt about what China has become. The People's Republic of China today features the entire syndrome of Fascist traits. Given the differences that result from a different history and a different culture, the political system that governs the China of today is Fascist in all but name. For the West that acknowledgment carries consequences. China, unless diverted by internal political and economic dislocation, will assiduously pursue its status and irredentist goals – in an enterprise that eventually must clash with the interests of the West.

What transpired in China exemplifies the continuities implicit in Fascism. Fascism is not simply a collection of doctrinal beliefs or public practices. It is a classic response to the imperatives of our time. It is a response to economic backwardness and/or status deprivation, as well as collective humiliation. It is the answer to a search for a current acknowledgment of distinction and a rehabilitation of a mythic past. Its traces are, and will continue to be, found in a variety of places. It is found in the posturing of Vladimir Putin and his irredentist efforts to restore his nation's "near afar" – those territories that had once been integral parts of the community. It is to be seen in Russia's abandonment of collective, for private property, rights. It is evident in the general allowance of the market to establish rational pricing and wage policies. It is evident in the control of labor and of public and private communication. It is apparent in the state sponsorship and management of education – and the insistence on the identification of the individual with the community.

Although there have been some who have sought to capture the continuities of Fascism in a flow of literature from the Fascist period that had been translated into Russian – the effort has come to very little. The continuity of Fascism is not to be found in the transmission of Fascist ideas through its doctrinal literature. Fascist continuities are the common consequence of late developers responding to a set of imperative demands arising from the surrounding environment. In such challenging environments, Fascism spontaneously makes an appearance. The major difficulty turns on our inability to identify those critical contingencies that give predictable rise to Fascist response.

The purpose all this serves is to suggest something of the behaviors to be expected from the subject systems. How much of an advantage that provides is difficult to say with conviction, but it does suggest that Russia's irredentist moves in Ukraine, and possibly in the Baltic states, are serious and pose a major concern for Western industrialized democracies.

China's end goal is its restoration as a Central Kingdom. Beijing will pursue that goal with application and special determination. So informed, the West must maintain its security forces to act as a counterweight to China's assertiveness. Systems such as these are prepared to risk confrontation with opponents of objectively greater power in order to achieve their purpose. The history of Italian Fascism tells us nothing if it does not tell us that these systems are prepared to face opponents far more powerful than they – in pursuit of chosen purpose.

Tracing Fascist continuities is instructive in many ways. It prepares us for possible futures – and supplies a perspective on the past that is more illuminating than any available alternative.

If your account of the "Fascist epoch" is accepted, what does it imply for the immediate present or the foreseeable future?

Acknowledging that social science is not a predictive occupation, social scientists do attempt reasoned speculations on the future. Such speculations are to be found in almost any academic treatment of contemporary events. There are regular efforts to draw out the implications of some simple or complex behavior on the part of one or another individual or state actor. Academicians who have studied Fascism have done no less. Some of the speculations are plausible and others implausible. It is largely left to the discipline to make those determinations. The difficulty lies in the fact that making such a determination may take a considerable length of time. The plausibility of any account may not be immediately evident or politically tolerable. Social science offers only plausible truths. It is a very informal discipline.

As far as the present account is concerned, its acceptability must rest on its intrinsic persuasiveness. How does it fare in comparison with other candidate accounts? Should it survive, we are then prepared to consider its implications.

The central claim of the account under scrutiny is that Italian Fascism provides us the paradigm instance of a reactive revolution, ignited by a people's deep sense of humiliation, a sense of humiliation that, in turn, fuels a program of accelerated economic and industrial development under the authoritarian auspices of a single party state. The account further suggests that a similar set of incentives will tend to engender a political arrangement sharing some or all of the properties of the paradigm. The cases of Arab and African socialism are offered in support of such a contention, and the instance of the People's Republic of China is extended as a kind of confirmation.

What seems clear is that rapid economic development in the twentieth century could not be pursued in a liberal democratic political environment. All of the polities that successfully developed in the last century conducted the drive to economic and industrial development under authoritarian modalities. South Korea, Taiwan, and Singapore achieved their respective levels of development under authoritarian governments. That they did not assume overtly Fascist traits was probably the consequence of the contemporary, collateral support of advanced industrial systems, either Britain or the United States. Such developing systems, freed of the threat of external enemies, could devote all their domestic energy to programs of economic growth and sophistication. Granted that, it could be argued that any community in the twenty-first century, finding itself suffering the impostures of foreign threat, might very well seek recourse to Fascist modalities. There are sectors in Africa or Latin America where such possibilities exist and where we might, once again, see the rise of Fascist powers. Subject to the demographic and resource base, supportive foreign alliances, and circumambient political stability, the survival and success of any such Fascist systems would depend on the qualities of their respective leaderships.

That the future might see Fascist systems arise in Europe proper is very unlikely because all the members of the European Union have largely completed the economic modernization of which they are capable. Moreover, it is most improbable that a European population that still harbors the recent memory of the Second World War would venture on yet another Fascist adventure. It is most unlikely that a Fascist movement would be anything other than a curiosity in contemporary Europe.

I have argued in several places that a fascistoid movement was likely in a Russia struggling out of the humiliating collapse of the Soviet Union. Although lacking some of the defining traits of Fascism, the present system in Russia is sufficiently similar to allow the judgment that the drive to restore its lost geographic integrity is serious – and any action by the North Atlantic Treaty Organization that Moscow might construe as fundamentally opposed to that purpose – could precipitate conflict, the consequences of which would be totally unpredictable.

Much the same might be said of the People's Republic of China. Its Fascist traits are unmistakable; and the implications for its conduct equally apparent. The deployment of Western military assets along the Chinese periphery, where Beijing seeks to incorporate "lost territories," is extremely hazardous. Directly involving Japan in the East China Sea, and the United States in the Sea of Japan adjacent to Korea, the future is uncertain and dangerous.

The analysis offers some suggestions with respect to the Middle East. As proposed, for a time, fascistoid movements flourished in the region. In North Africa, Nasser's revolution was a marginal success until his death. Thereafter, the system devolved into a traditional authoritarian arrangement. The jihadist movements that have arisen to fill in the political space vacated by Arab Socialism, have precious little that is Fascist about them. They are pathological mass movements, animated by a politicized religion (rather than a suitable, secular faith), that offer very little other than apocalyptic violence, mass murder, and the promise of a retrograde caliphate that would embody the stolid rule of medieval dysfunction. With the failure of Arab Socialism, the revolutionaries of the Middle East pursue the genocidal extermination of Jews, and the mass destruction of "inferiors," in order to restore a lost civilization.

Without the availability of a serious notion of an extended Fascist epoch, the present time appears more confused and chaotic than it is. The notion of a Fascist epoch allows us to classify political systems, anticipate something of their behavior, and dismiss any expectation of universal liberal democratic arrangements taking place any time in the foreseeable future. As long as there are communities convinced that their political and cultural inferiority is an imposed consequence of "imperialist" imposture – one or another form of "fascist," or still more threatening reaction, can only be expected.

All of this is reasoned speculation, but that is what writing or talking about international politics is all about.

Much of what you say is cast in terms of broad generalities that defy intersubjective confirmation. How can we have confidence that what you say is true?

Unhappily, there are very few claims advanced by social scientists that can pretend to the level of truth common in the mathematical sciences. In recognition of the informal character of social science, there are those who have attempted its remedy. "Behaviorists," among academic social scientists, have attempted the employ the standard procedures of the more formal sciences in the study of associated human behavior. The result has been to attempt the experimental study of complex political behavior. An effort is made to study human beings using experimental procedures, randomly selecting test subjects and subjecting them to the impact of an experimental variable – comparing the results to control groups. The successes using such methods are applicable to those groups from which probability samples had been selected. The results, restricted to the populations from which samples were drawn, are highly credible – but given the character of the experiments hardly applicable (without significant qualification) to the broader populations with which theoretical social scientists tend to deal. The choice is to produce credible claims that characteristically apply to relatively small populations, or tender broader claims that are less credible. It becomes immediately apparent that neither historians nor "theoretical" social scientists can pretend to do "experimental social science." Often the subject of their inquiry involves entire historic epochs or millions of subjects. Since no one has suggested a method by which one might experimentally study millions of subjects over decades, historians and social scientists conduct their business in traditional manner. They proceed to formulate an explanatory account of a chosen period or a given population, based on the best available evidence, aspiring to plausibility rather than experimental confirmation.

"Confirmation" or "verification" in the non-experimental sciences comes in a variety of forms. Some "confirmation" is sought in either surviving documentation covering simple or complex events, or in explicit ideas that are found in the doctrinal literature of a select period. There are occasions in which consistency is sought in the recorded behaviors of historic actors compared with their expressed intention. The results produced by these kinds of confirmation are not comparable to those we expect in physics. History and social science are not that sort of inquiry. In history and theoretical social science, we do not seek impeccable truths, but evidenced plausibilities – with some of the plausibilities more plausible than others. For social scientists it is often the case that a "truth" is a plausibility more plausible than any available alternative.

Sometimes the select plausibility "illuminates" a complex and obscure sequence of historical events. At other times, it suggests an interesting line of inquiry. On occasion, a particular plausible account anticipates events. All these considerations render one account intrinsically more preferable to others.

The informality surrounding confirmation in history and social science leaves both their practitioners as well as their audiences dissatisfied. In the attempt to allay, at least in part, the cognitive concerns of both the practitioner as well as his audience, both historians and social scientists will very carefully confirm the authenticity of documents involved in the subject matter. They will provide relevant, empirical evidence as available. None of that, unhappily, will make historiography or social science anything other than an informal discipline. In substance, what they will attempt is the collection of verifiable empirical evidence wherever possible in the effort to offset skepticism, seek coherence among the constituent elements considered, and package the collection in clear and comprehensible prose. Writing an account of a complex sequence of events taking place over time is something like producing a work of art. It is filled with sentiment – with approval and disapproval – with enthusiasm or with rejection. The difference is that neither history nor social science, in principle, allows the practitioner artistic license in presenting his findings to the public. The historian and the social scientist are charged with the responsibility of delivering a true account of events that involve the lives of millions of actors. It is an onerous responsibility of which every serious historian and social scientist is fully aware.

Books by A. James Gregor

- A Survey of Marxism: Problems in Philosophy and the Theory of History
- Contemporary Radical Ideologies: Totalitarian Thought in the Twentieth Century
- Interpretations of Fascism
- The Ideology of Fascism: The Rationale of Totalitarianism
- Italian Fascism and Developmental Dictatorship
- The Fascist Persuasion in Radical Politics
- Young Mussolini and the Intellectual Origins of Fascism
- Mussolini's Intellectuals: Fascist Social and Political Thought
- The Search for Neofascism: The Use and Abuse of Social Science
- Giovanni Gentile: Philosopher of Fascism
- The Faces of Janus: Marxism and Fascism in the Twentieth Century
- Marxism, Fascism and Totalitarianism:; Chapters in the Intellectual History of Radicalism
- Totalitarianism and Political Religion: An Intellectual History
- A Place in the Sun: Marxism and Fascism in China's Long Revolution
- Ideology and Development: Sun Yat-sen and the Economic History of Taiwan
- Marxism, China, and Development: Reflections on Theory and Reality
- Marxism and the Making of China: A Doctrinal History